I CAN'T DO WHAT?

Voices of Pathfinding Women

by

Barbara Hutmacher MacLean

Pathfinder Publishing
Ventura, California

I CAN'T DO WHAT?

Published by:
Pathfinder Publishing of California
458 Dorothy Avenue
Ventura, CA 93003
(805) 642-9278

Library of Congress Cataloging-in-Publication Data

MacLean, Barbara hutmacher, 1926-
    I can't do what? : voices of pathfinding women / by Barbara
Hutmacher MacLean.
        p. cm.
    Includes index.
    ISBN 0-934793-62-X (pbk.)
    1. Women in the professions—United States—Biography. I. Title.
HD6054.2.U6M33   1996
331.4"092"273—dc20
[B]   96-28005
                                                        CIP

DEDICATION

To my mother, Betty, and my daughters, Beth, Cary, and Jessica

ACKNOWLEDGMENTS

Family, friends, and strangers contributed in unique ways to this book. I hope not to miss anyone, but failure is probably built in because of the many who did help.

First on the list are the women who make up this book. They never failed me. Thanks to Bernard Belonski; Donna Maloney; Wilfred Woods; the staff at the national offices of the American Medical Association and the American Bar Association; Carolyn Meiselbach at Catalyst, a women's advocacy group, and the Catalyst Information Center; Major Anita Minnifield; my aunt, Alice Wall; Pamela Amoss; Charles and Helga Frankel; Steve DeForest; Don and Joyce Buddington; Arlene Jackson; Joey and Gene Connell; members of my family, Beth Hutmacher, Jessica Schneider, Cary Bayley, Dave Hutmacher, and Clay Hutmacher, who read, made suggestions and fed and housed us.

Thanks to my friends who shared their career histories before this book took a different direction. We meet for lunches once a month and keep each other excited about this phase of our lives: Pamela Amoss, Rita Clark, Terry Craig, Marlene Curtis, Mary Perkins, Betty Shreve, Jean Payne Vick, and Naomi Wood.

Thanks as well to Wenatchee Public Library and North Central Washington Regional Library personnel who found answers I didn't have and books I needed: and to Rich Morneau who took on three daring computer rescues at inconvenient times.

Special thanks to Fraser. He made travel arrangements, sat in on interviews and expressed his enthusiasm of what he heard, did the photography, read early drafts, and a whole lot more.

CONTENTS

Acknowledgments
Introduction   7
1. Faith Hubley   17
2. Iona Hardy Campagnolo   33
3. Anne Wexler   47
4. Violet Anderson Hilbert   58
5. Katherine Woodruff Fanning   66
6. Florence Crim Robinson, Ph.D.   79
7. Denise Scott Brown   96
8. Patricia McGowan Wald   111
9. June Lee Biedler, Ph.D.   128
10. Caroline Herzenberg, Ph.D.   140
11. Gloria W. Heath   151
12. Gen. Evelyn Foote, (Ret.)   163
13. Ah Quon McElrath   179
14. Jean Lee Payne   187
15. Muriel Siebert   198
16. Palma Formica, M.D.   212
17. Afterwords   228
Index   232

"Forget conventialisms; forget what the world will say, whether you are in your place or out of your place; think your best thoughts, speak your best words, do your best works, looking (only) to your own conscience for approval."

Susan B. Anthony

1863

INTRODUCTION

"I understand you've written a book," she said. "What about?"

About women, I said—now in their 60s and 70s and heroines, writers of women's history, vanguard of a massive social change in America. But not many know about them because these women worked for personal reasons, not for fame. Besides, careers in the military, or law, or medicine, are not at all unusual for women these days. What makes this group of women unique is, they got there first, during a time when women didn't think beyond jobs as teachers, actresses, in offices, as nurses, or, if sufficiently decorative and personable, pushing carts along the aisles of airplanes.

But first off, I'd say I haven't written this book at all, I just put it together. Sixteen remarkable women related their stories. I did not attempt to analyze their accomplishments nor to interpret these past what is required to establish their successes in their fields. Professional journals speak to the minutiae of professions. The person and the life behind the achievements concerned me.

Fourteen of these 20th century pioneers were born between the adoption of universal women's suffrage in 1920 and the early Depression years, a miserable decade in our history that began in 1929. Two women are older.

These 16 are among the first generation of women to achieve success in non-traditional careers. They could fairly be said to have launched a working world of open choices that never before existed for women. Girls today grow up believing they can choose any career that interests them and have no idea that hasn't always been so. But in 1920, for example, only three percent of American lawyers were women. Fifty years later, 10 percent of first year law students were women; by 1989, 40 percent of law students were women. The number of women physicians rose from nine percent in 1971 to 22 percent in 1981 and, by 1995, almost half of first-year med students were females. Women above secretarial rank don't show up on Bureau of Labor Statistics until 1972 when 14 percent of managers were reported to be women; by 1994, that soared to 43 percent. Equitable salaries didn't become an issue until 1963 when Congress passed the Equal Pay Act, introduced by Rep. Helen Gahagan Douglas of California. This specified wages be the same for employees performing the same kind of work. Though unenforceable, it became the first federal law against sex discrimination and recognition of women as wage earners.

Looking around at what women are achieving today, it's hard to believe that society's ideas on women's place changed so radically in the latter third of the 20th century. The history of female subservience dates back to the settling of America. English colonists brought with them a patriarchal society based on political and religious traditions and saw no reason to change what worked just fine, at least for men, when they switched countries. Their comfortable status quo didn't begin to shake for a couple of centuries.

In the 17th and 18th centuries women's involvements had embraced only family and church. Then came the Industrial Revolution bringing with it radical change. Home production moved to workshops and then to factories. Men left their houses to work, giving wives a refreshing autonomy for what went on at home. Factories, because of their need for labor pools, concentrated people in cities, which had a lot to do with everything that happened from then on.

Between the Civil War and World War I, a significant number of women joined the labor force in factories and offices. Most often young and single, they were likely to be daughters of city-dwelling immigrants. Since women were perpetual newcomers in the job market, they took the lowest level jobs at the lowest pay. Highly desirable qualifications to employers.

But once again, society—men—changed the rules. During the Depression, women were urged to stay home and leave the jobs remaining to family "breadwinners." Urged might be an understatement. Women made up three-quarters of the federal workers asked to resign; most of the nation's school systems wouldn't hire married women and if women married, they had to quit. War reversed that thinking. In 1942, women were invited into defense plants and government offices. During World War II, over six million women worked outside the home for the first time in their lives. But from day one, it was understood. When the men came home, they'd go home too.

After the war, America became pretty much a Doris Day movie until the 1960s.

Looking back, the first significant event of the women's movement may have been President John Kennedy's appointment of the Commission on the Status of Women in 1961. Though the Commission didn't change society's rules relative to women, it had a singular and major achievement: providing a focus for women who began creating their own network of communication.

Other mile markers in contemporary women's history included:

- Publication of "The Feminine Mystique" by Betty Friedan in 1963;
- Formation of the National Organization for Women (NOW) in 1966;
- President Lyndon B. Johnson's 1967 signing of an order banning sex discrimination in federal jobs, and another removing restrictions that kept women in the military from advancing beyond the rank of colonel;
- The 1972 Supreme Court decision, Roe vs Wade, which legalized abortion through the first trimester of pregnancy.

Thus, by the time the 1980s arrived, young women faced a range of possibilities very different from that of their mothers and grandmothers. Also relevant was the birth control pill, approved for sale in 1960. If a woman could control her own reproductive life, she might aim at a career few women of the previous generations would have even considered.[1]

But, in spite of the roadblocks at mid-century, a number of women had already hurdled them and that is the story here: Women, now in their 60s and 70s, successful in the male-dominated professions they chose.

I call women who walked in cold to a hostile workplace M's, or Models; models, by dictionary definition [2], being a standard or example for imitation or comparison. M's were exactly that. They came in without role models and usually no mentors. They made up their professional lives as they went along and grew to be very good at that. Their education included leveling pay inequities, speaking out in all-male gatherings, promoting themselves, talking to lawyers when necessary.

So that was the object of the search—successful women who came early to non-traditional fields.

I found them by various means. Friends in the same professions came up with recommendations. The Army, American Bar and American Medical Associations offered suggestions. I spent many hours at the local library, cross-referencing Marquis' "Who's Who" entries. In some fields where women and men both operated, such as music and journalism, the women selected functioned in traditionally male sectors: a composer and conductor rather than performer; a newspaper editor, not the editor of a lifestyle section.

Letters describing the concept, outlining the questions, asking for a meeting, came next. Acceptances at a ratio of about five to one were encouraging as to the value of the project.

Trying to set up an interview schedule with some kind of reasonable itinerary proved unexpectedly complicated. These women attended conferences in Oslo, were on panels in Paris and St. Louis. They performed in New York and spoke in Denver.

But arrangements were finally made and the interviews turned out to be even more fascinating than could be imagined. Their backgrounds ranged from extreme poverty to privileged. Teachers, parents, and grandparents proved gratifyingly influential in many lives. Many of these high-achievers grew up appreciating the value of books and remained devout readers. All somehow knew, inherently, that all things were possible with sufficient effort. That strong work ethic was probably the only factor common to everyone.

What became particularly fascinating, was how they came to their professions. Only one of the 16 women interviewed knew from childhood what she wanted to do for the rest of her life. The careers of the others simply evolved, usually from an accidental first step.

For instance, the first civil service exam Jean Payne took was in corrections. She passed and went from there. Evelyn "Pat" Foote happened to talk to a woman Army officer at a time when her job wasn't going where she wanted to go. Iona Campagnolo's rich political career grew out of garden club activism.

M's, because of their generation and American society at that time, graduated from high school with clear guidelines to adult life. They would go to college, earn a degree in a field considered appropriate for women. If they didn't meet their future husbands in college, they would work until they did. After marriage, most quit their jobs, settled down—in the terminology of the time—and began producing the children a society deprived by Depression and war welcomed. When their children went off to school, women were expected to fill the space with community service—Scout leader, hospital volunteer, membership in a club supporting a worthy cause.

But along the way, beginning in the mid-1950s and continuing through the 1960s and 1970s, a significant number of women independently decided there was more in life than houses, husbands, and children and they wanted a share of it. Was this because of college educations and unused knowledge? A growing

11

focus in society on personal fulfillment? Easy to get divorces? Politicization? Ambition wasn't anything we'd learned at our mothers' knees.

How strange it all looks now. What my mother wanted out of life was security: a "nice" house in a nice neighborhood with nice things in it. Though she'd worked in an office until her marriage, she wanted a college education for her two children. Why seemed understood by all. College would lead to a career for her son and a good marriage for her daughter.

There is, I believe, some law of science that says, basically, what you think will happen when you launch an object, isn't what does happen once that object is set in motion. College didn't guarantee we'd just get better at what our mothers did, be happier, more fulfilled, college gave us ideas. College coinciding with great changes in society produced new perspectives on our future.

In a way, this is ironic. My daughters—and women colleagues of their age—went from college to career and now daydream, longingly, about my mother's way of life.

But, for whatever reasons, the M's struck out into unknown territory and took what they found.

This project proved fascinating. I loved just about every part of it. Meeting these women was inspiring and a privilege. One reason I found their stories so engrossing was that they provided an affirmation of my own life.

Like so many of the women in this book, I'd begun working when my youngest went off to school. I'd married halfway through college, given birth to five children in quick succession, and become a housewife.

When I was 35, my husband's job took us to an unfamiliar community on the other side of the country. My children were in school. I didn't join anything. I hung out in front of the television, got fat and depressed, and tried, unsuccessfully, to choreograph the lives of my husband and children.

This bad time coincided with major events in our country: the civil rights movement and soon afterwards, the assassination of several political leaders, heroes to many. Growing within me was an enormous need to do something, but what that was I had no idea.

Talking to the women in this book, I learned they'd had similar needs. How reassuring. Also that the frowns and admonitions of neighbors and parents to a mother/wife working were standard to them also. Oh, the guilt at bailing out. Women are so good at that. Women then were expected to stay home and take care of things. Everyone's things. And then you got old and then you died.

I ended up in journalism as the result of a chance remark at a party. The chamber of commerce president said the editor of the paper in nearby Richmond, Virginia, called. He wondered if our neighbor knew anyone interested in reporting news in our community for his newspaper.

I still remember grabbing that offhand remark as if it were a lifeline and at that stage, it could have been.

I started out at 25 cents a published column inch and spent 75 cents per column inch on gas to get it. But I loved finding out what was going on and writing about it. Over the next 30 years I worked hard enough at this to do what I wanted to do in my life.

It was easy for me compared to some. Many of the women I met had overcome formidable difficulties. They lost jobs and elections. They divorced. They survived life-threatening illnesses, deaths of spouses, siblings and children. To me, their message was no matter what the odds, don't be discouraged. Persevere. You, too, can do it.

Though the gender barriers in the world of work may be down, obstacles to achieving our personal best remain. These women prove whatever these may be, they are not insurmountable. Anyone needing a shot of inspiration can find it here. I did. When my writing wasn't going well, I'd get out the interviews and read through them once again. Initially, it was to look for the transposed or missing letter, the misspelling that always gets through no matter how many times something is read. But after a time, I just read them, mainly to get a boost. They'd continued on in spite of everything. So would I.

I'd begun this book for very personal reasons. I needed a project.

Four years earlier, at the end of 1991, I'd retired. Six months later, my husband, Fraser, and I bought a boat in England. For the next three years, we cruised the rivers and canals of England during the summer and spent winters at our house in the foothills of Washington state's Cascade Mountains.

Before returning home that last autumn, we'd left the boat at a marina. A few months later, it sold. That had been the idea but it proved, unexpectedly, as unsettling a change for me as the cross-country move half a lifetime earlier. Somehow, planning to go away, leaving home-centered responsibilities for six months, then getting resettled once again, took up head space and energy. After the boat went, I woke every morning wondering what I could do until it was time to go back to bed. Eventually I asked the right questions: What skill did I have? How could that be used to fill a day with measurable accomplishments? After a lot of sifting and sorting, the plan evolved of writing a book about high-achieving women of my generation. I knew they were out there. After all, I'd written about such women for newspapers for years. The original idea was to compare the early options for careers in a small community, my own, with those offered in a large urban center, Seattle.

But, this book, like my children, did not turn out as planned. A literary agent suggested expanding the geographical boundaries. To do that I looked at specific professions. From there, came the concept of talking to women who'd chosen to pursue careers in male-dominated fields.

I'd planned to address retirement in the book, but not a single M had retired, not in the conventional meaning of that word. If they didn't actually show up at the office every weekday, they all remained active in their fields—writing, speaking, or serving on related boards. When the question of future plans came up, the

14

only acknowledgment of retirement seemed to be a vague idea of cutting back at some indefinite future time. That probably is the way to go. Floyd Schmoe's secret to a long and rich life is taped to the side of my printer. I would have liked Floyd to have been Florence, but his motto is still worth passing along: "Always have something important to do tomorrow, something to look forward to."

Throughout my journalism career, which almost from the beginning focused on people and their personal stories, I'd go into an interview with certain expectations of what would be told, related to what I knew about that individual. And what I heard always was different.

That proved true again, sixteen times.

1 In 1960, 37.7 percent of American women were employed; by 1993, 57.9 percent of women worked. In 1970, .05 percent of working women earned $50,000-$74,000 annually; by 1991, that percentage rose to 2.0. All amounts are given in 1992 dollars. Figures from Statistical Abstract of the United States, 1994 edition.

2 Webster's Encyclopedic Unabridged Dictionary of the English Language: Portland House.

1

Faith Hubley, filmmaker, painter, animator;
born 1924; president Hubley Studio, New
York; senior critic Yale School of Art; three
Oscars, seven nominations; numerous international film festival honors.

A week or so before the interview with Faith Hubley, PBS—
KCTS in Seattle—showed a documentary, "Animated
Women," which featured a lengthy segment on Hubley
and her work. What seemed most amazing was how anyone could
imagine, then create art in that crazy yet telling form we usually
think of as cartoons. Her films were not the Saturday morning,
Disney variety. In "Tall Time Tales," she'd imagined time moving in circles rather than forward, then created fanciful shapes with
human and animal movements, bits of dialogue, sounds, and frag-
ments of music to tell the story.[1] Dream stuff, child's art, used to
deliver fresh perspectives of accepted beliefs.

Hubley lived and worked in an apartment building in
Riverdale which, she'd said on the phone, was just another name
for the elegant parts of the Bronx. We checked in with an atten-
dant in the lobby then took an elevator to the 12th floor. An outside balcony with a waist-high rail passed a half dozen doors to
end at Hubley's. She led the way through the entry, living, dining,
and kitchen areas, past her office and cutting room, to her

studio. That was bedroom-sized with a band of windows where, standing up, you could see the Hudson River below and the black cliffs called The Palisades along the opposite bank.

After deciding we should sit around a table, Hubley twirled herself into a small package to fit a small chair, fitting her legs under her in places mine hadn't visited in 20 years. Her hair was about the same gray as her warm-ups. She wore patterned socks and no shoes. Her skin was smooth over high cheekbones and a strong jaw. She laughed often, squinting dark eyes. Like her art, Hubley proved animated, charming, and an original.

In 1955 she and her husband, John Hubley, collaborated on their first film. Since his death in 1977, she'd worked alone, turning out an animated short every year.

She'd just completed her 1995 project, "Rainbows of Hawaii," and already, the wall opposite her had become the drawing board for the next. After a vertical line of numbers written with a felt pen were pinned pieces of paper, about 4-inches square, with the ideas so far. These included "My Universe Inside Out," "Global Mind," "I and the Universe Are One," "Celebrate," and "Go West."

Behind Hubley's chair, books on Miro, Bonnard, Matisse, volumes of mythology and arts of the world, filled floor-to-ceiling, wall-to-wall bookcases.

A painting in progress, as abstract and colorful as her film images, leaned against an easel in the corner. Pinned to the wall nearby was a hand-drawn calendar and a New York Times clipping of April 5, 1995, headlined "Animation As Fine Art In Faith Hubley's Work."

The conversation began in this way: "I'm an independent and animated filmmaker. I make one film a year and I commission myself—that's how I describe independent. I decide what it is that I need to say, and once the theme is decided, I pretend I'm fully financed and very rich. That works wonders because the beginning parts of the process are not expensive.

"I learned this trick from the great filmmakers because money has always been a problem in this industry. They told me, 'When you're not working, you pretend you have money to make a film and you plan it. That's because if an angel walks up to you and gives you budget for a film and you don't have three films ready to go, you're stuck.' But I prefer having just one. This is what I can do, comfortably, and I just keep going, one way or the other. And if I end up in debt, which I usually do, I eventually pay that off and acquire new debts, pretty much like the government." She laughed. "Deficit financing will get you a long, long way."

Hawaiian mythology and oceanic art inspired her latest film. "I chose the subject," She said, "because I knew very little about it. And I figured if I knew little about it, there must be others.

"Hawaii's indigenous people are even more neglected than our mainland indigenous people and I can tell you a funny story about that. One year, at UCLA (University of California at Los Angeles), they had money for Native Americans left over. A bunch of Hawaiian students applied and were told they didn't qualify.

"So these things combined, plus I just love the art that comes out of those beautiful islands. I also try to do things that are useful." She grinned: "I think I make films so I can be a perennial student. I love learning, that's why I live. When I stop learning, I'll go to the next place.

"My films are primarily visual experiences. There are very few words. I don't like it that in our current culture, we're so unbalanced, we have to read everything. People go to museums. What do they do? They rent little earphones and march around in an obedient way."

Hubley's films unfold according to a very personal timetable. "I start (thinking of the next film) in the spring because I'm really a bird, though I look like a person. It's all very, very seasonal. I finish in March or April, but since February, I've been honing in on the next project. By the time I've finished, I'm clearly, mentally, into the next project."

After the story ideas, come the research, story visualization, and drawings and painting around which the film will be developed. The solitary, sacred part of the process, she called that.

Solitary creativity is followed by collaboration with the composer for the score, with sound development, and finally with animators and camera.

Unlike most artists, she admitted to no dry spells, no artistic blocks. "We're meant to have a continuum," she said, "and if you stop it's very scary. The motor runs down. The cells dry up. Then you do that terrible thing of wondering if you are any good or not. My work is my religion, my commitment. I do the best I can and don't, in any way, try to evaluate my work. No more than I would say, 'I'm sorry I had all these children. Why don't you all go away and do something else while I decide whether you're any good or I'm any good.' It's like breathing and I've been this way all of my life, though it was hard for me to get to it because there were many obstacles. I think sometimes when there are obstacles, one achieves a way of working.

"My husband, John, would go into a terrible mental depression when we finished a film and I would have to pull him out of his depression and rev us up for the next work. While I miss him very, very much, and wish he were here, a part of me is happy not to have that extra burden. (Antonin) Dvorak, who was the son of a butcher, had a difficult life with loss and tragedy. But he never stopped composing. He could no more stop composing than he could stop breathing.

"My theory is that as long as you don't step back and try to evaluate, you're all right. If you do, chances are you'll think it's terrible, and then you'll try to do something different—you'll get consumed with fashion. 'Oh, I can't repeat myself.' I see nothing wrong with repeating oneself. I love mythology so a lot of my films are about mythology. A man said to me, 'Why do your films look basically alike?' And I said, 'Because I make them. I'm not in the cloning business. Style doesn't interest me.' 'Well,' he said, 'you certainly make it hard for those of us who have to look at the same things over and over.' I said, 'I didn't ask you to look.'"

My own response was absolutely opposite of her critic. The "Animated Women" documentary included two of her short films.

A major first impression had been, how could anyone come up with two films of such different artistic concepts? And later, after seeing all of her films,[2] that initial response remained. What an amazing, multi-layered imagination those films reflected.

Hubley's concepts were uniquely self-realized. She did not go to Australia to look at aboriginal art before she did "Cloudland," (1993) nor to Hawaii to research her latest film. She went to the library.

"Any money I have, I use to make my films," she said. "I am not Hawaiian. I never will be Hawaiian. I'm not going to pretend to be Hawaiian.

"What I need to find out, what I'm fundamentally interested in—ancient culture—isn't going to be there anyway. It would be lovely if I were wealthy and could afford to go to these places, but I can't and I've grown accustomed to going without." Again her laughter.

"I love the way I work. In terms of art appreciation, I don't get that much more from being face to face. I must ingest everything and recreate it through my own eyes. I really don't feel deprived.

"I did a film on the rain forest[3] and—this is an example of how we can't let our ego and vanity influence us—I got scared someone would say, 'How do you know anything about the rain forest if you've never been there?' And I had a little money left over that year so I made an economy trip to the rain forest, just so I could say, 'I've been to the rain forest.'" Laugh break: "And nobody every asked."

She'd gone to Trinidad with a tour aimed at bird watchers: "All the bird-watching people got up at 5 in the morning and walked around looking and listening to the birds. And there was one cave they were all afraid of because there was supposed to be a big snake in the cave. I've always been snake-phobic, so I made myself, with slow steps, walk to the cave. I stood there for half an hour. I looked at the flora and fauna and trees and then I said to the snake, 'I'm not afraid of you any more. Goodbye.' Very therapeutic."

What talents go into making films? Extraordinary and continuing discipline and a great love of the medium, Hubley said. "You just find a way to do it. It took me 30 years to find my way to the right place. Part of that was accident. But what do we know about accidents? I knew I wanted to do this, if it were possible—and I didn't think it would be possible for all the reasons people think you can't do everything you want to do in life. And, of course, we know you can."

People should love their work, she said. And finding work that is a pleasure is not all that difficult, providing loving work is separated from money. "That's what I tell young people—or old people or anyone—you just arrange everything accordingly."

Hubley's career in films began when she was 18. "I started in live action in Hollywood—regular movies—because I wanted to know how things worked and I could earn while I learned. During World War II, I got a job as messenger. Normally, the boys got their chance with this training. The studios would never, never hire girls, but the war came and they had no choice. So I was in a group of young women who made entry at that point. I chose Columbia Studios. I wanted to stay long enough to be first editor on a film. And in the studio system, if I made it by 50, I'd be lucky.

"When I look back I think I was smart, but I didn't think I was then. I'd never stay at anything more than a year because I thought by that time, I'd have the technical rudiments, and I wanted to keep learning."

After learning to cut sound effects, music, and how to be a script clerk, she left the studio system to work on a documentary. "A whole series of films were made right after World War II when for half a minute people were idealistic," she said.

"When Eddie Albert came back from the war, he and his wife, Margo, wanted to use their talent and money to educate the young." Their idea resulted in a classic film, "Human Reproduction," designed to teach junior high school boys and girls about their bodies and human reproduction, and which would dispel any nonsense they'd picked up along the way.

"It took four months to get enough parents to agree to sign a piece of paper allowing their children to be in this so-called dirty film," Hubley recalled. "After the shooting, Eddie Albert hired John Hubley—who worked at UPA (United Productions of America) and later became my husband—to do the animation. And Johnny did this wonderful abstract, like a moving painting, of the inside of a woman's body. It looked like a Georgia O'Keeffe skull and was very colorful and aesthetically beautiful, and kids could have watched it from now until the cows came home.

"And I looked at what Johnny was doing and what I was doing—cutting the film, splicing and hand-coding, and working 18 hours a day. He brings in his art. He drifts out. He's on to his next project.

"He doesn't have to deal with all these personalities. I'm stuck in the cutting room and all the guys in the lab think I'm some weirdo. They'd hang out and say, 'Oh, there's the lady doing the dirty film...'

"I worked and worked and worked. I thought, I'm not doing what I really want."

She left and went to Europe. She and her roommate, a film editor she'd met when they were both messengers at Columbia, had saved enough money to take a year off. Hubley explained, "We decided since we hadn't gone to college, we deserved a year abroad. I spent three months of that at the Cinematique in Paris. I offered to work and they let me."

After Paris, she did not return to Hollywood but, instead, moved back to New York where her first job was on a film about the Harlem Globetrotters basketball team.

"I edited the film like it was a ballet and Alex North wrote a wonderful score. Then John was in town. I wanted Johnny to help me design a montage for it. He said, 'How about chalk drawings on the street?' And we got kids to do chalk drawings on the street."

The film, James Wong Howe's "Go Man Go," done in the early 1950s, remained a favorite of Hubley's. "It was beautiful to watch. I went to see it on 42nd Street. A bunch of really tough people loved it. And whatever they say about 'We make terrible, crummy films because that's what people want,' it's just not true. People want the best and often they don't get a chance to choose."

When Hubley and Faith met again on the basketball team documentary, they'd been friends for nearly 10 years. "We all wanted to do a film against racism," she said. "This was before the civil rights movement and we had many meetings and talked a great deal about the film.

"I loved Johnny's work and I used to tease him. 'You're scared,' I'd say. 'Why don't you quit where you are and make a film of your own?' He'd say, 'I can't. I have a family.'"

Previously an art director at Disney studios, John Hubley had been among many participants in a bitter 1941 strike against the studio. He left to become one of the founders of UPA and returned there after service in World War II. That ended when he was added to the film industry's roll of suspected Communists or Communist sympathizers called before Sen. Joseph McCarthy's Un-American Activities Commission in the 1950s. John Hubley subsequently was blacklisted.

Why? "The individual stories of the McCarthy era are of little importance," his wife said. "The question is, how did we end up with a McCarthy with a blacklist embraced by the moving pictures? It was more financial than political: 'Mirror, mirror, on the wall, who is the most beautiful of us all?' Much of it had to do with competition. Consider the case of Charlie Chaplin. And, in the end, everyone just said they were sorry..."

After John Hubley left UPA, he began making commercials. "At that point," she said, "the people who did the Broadway musical, 'Finian's Rainbow,' wanted to turn it into an animated film and hired Johnny to do the storyboard and direct their film.

"After a while, because Johnny could get stuck, they hired me to be his assistant because I had this reputation of being an on-time, on-budget lady. So I was like his caretaker: 'We have to start now.' 'We have to finish now.' 'We need to do everything today we said we would.' The film was never finished, but we fell in love and got married and I convinced him to move to New York."

Faith had been born in New York, to a father with a Polish-Russian heritage, a dentist, and a mother of Romanian descent. The Cinderella of their four offspring, her childhood was scarred by verbal and emotional abuse. She existed in a state of perpetual anger, believing herself ugly, unwanted, and inferior; often considering suicide which seemed her only escape.

"I grew up in Hells' Kitchen," Hubley said. "It was awful then and, other than clothing styles, it probably hasn't changed much. A girl named Nancy in eighth grade was a working prostitute and we all knew it. We certainly weren't stupid. We were street smart and serious thinkers. There was a librarian in grade school—Margaret M. Ward—who was wonderful and really important in my life. I wrote to her until she stopped writing back.

"She took us to the library, 54th Street and 10th Avenue, and said, 'Open those doors and there is the universe.

"'Anything you want is there. And it's free...' My last year in grade school, she gave me a string of pearls. I kept them for years. When I got older I used to wear them and pretend I was a Vassar student. When I was hired to be a messenger at Columbia Pictures, I lied and said I'd finished high school. I was well read and intelligent, precocious, and I always wore my pearls. People would say, 'Oh, did you go to Vassar?' And I couldn't carry the lie that far. I'd look down and say, 'The war came.'"

Though Hubley completed the academic requirements, she dropped out of high school before graduation. Her father had withheld papers required to pass hygiene which was a requisite. Not until a few years ago did she receive her high school diploma. By that time, she'd been awarded an honorary degree from Columbia College in Chicago. As David Pease, the dean of Yale School of Art where she is senior critic, noted, a high school diploma following a doctorate may have been a first.

I Can't Do What?

"I tell this story for a reason," Hubley said. "In a way we are addressing people who have not led regular lives—which is probably the overwhelming majority. One shouldn't be discouraged. So I went to the university of life and emerged a student."

When she left high school, she said, "I was scared and angry. I knew there was another world, but I didn't know where it was."

She moved to California, worked briefly in a defense plant and then as a waitress. Sure it was scary, an 18-year-old, living in unknown territory among strangers, but, she said, "I had no choice other than to be fearless."

She not only had no idea of her future, she did not really expect to live past 27. That was the age of her mother's brother when he committed suicide. Since childhood, she'd been told she was, like him, a sensitive misfit.

She was 20 when she left Columbia for Republic studios, home of the Westerns but, she said, "with an incredible music department. I worked freelance and made a lot of money. I was a music editor and assigned to (Leopold) Stokowski and (Anton) Rubinstein—who didn't talk to each other—for their recording of Rachmaninoff's Piano Concerto. I could follow the score and align the tracks and they both thought I was wonderful—probably because I was the medium between them.

"I also worked with George Antheil, the bad boy of music. He was a modern composer—dead now—who was coming into his own. He did the scores for Ben Hecht's films, including 'Spectre of the Rose.' Antheil was so disciplined in his work. It was from him that I learned discipline. The whole experience of working with Hecht, and with him, taught me how to be an independent."

Hubley would work for a time, save every cent she could and then quit to work on her education.

She said, "I read American literature and a lot of American history because I got skipped a lot in grade school and missed it, though I knew about the rest of the world.

"My first real painting teacher asked if I'd seen the work of Pierre Bonnard. I hadn't. She said, 'You paint just like him.' I probably didn't, but it was a great compliment. At some other time, she said, 'Have you studied Persian miniatures?' I said 'No, but I will,' and kept painting."

As for her marriage, after returning from Europe and meeting John Hubley once again on "Go Man Go," then "Finian's Rainbow," they fell in love and married. In the years that followed, the Hubleys made 21 films together and raised four children.

"The rest of it was pretty straightforward," Hubley said, "until I got cancer and that was pretty awful. And after cancer, Johnny died very unexpectedly, and then I went on with my cancer battle."

Doctors told her she had breast cancer in 1974. Surgery, radiation, chemotherapy, all the available treatments, followed.

"I had everything," Hubley said. "I don't think it was the everything that did it. It was the green glop.

"We had this Trinidadian housekeeper we all adored. A big, tough woman. She said, 'That chemo stuff isn't going to help you, that's going to make you sicker, my dear. I will bring you the green thing.' She would come with these greens she bought at the markets in the Bronx. Stuff I can't even name.

"She'd mix green, bitter herbs and say to me, 'This is your green voodoo drink and you drink a glass a day.' I don't know this didn't work. We know cancer is a mysterious disease. We know people in the rain forest don't get cancer.

"This battle with cancer went on for many years. I grew lots of lumps and made a lot of lumps go away. And one day, about 1984, I decided I was cured. My surgeon was also a wonderful writer and an excellent teacher. If I happened to be in for an examination and he had students, he'd bring them in and say, 'Now this is the lady who said she could cure herself. And don't forget there are such people and always let them do it.'"

I asked about her husband's death. "Johnny was a hypochondriac and the sad thing about hypochondriacs is that after awhile, no one listens to them. I certainly didn't. He'd had a little bit of a heart problem and it was recommended he have a heart bypass. It was simple, straightforward, except that when they operated, they found he had a damaged aorta, probably from birth, and he bled to death."

John Hubley was 63 when he died in 1977. The Hubleys' four children were then in their teens and early twenties.

Before his death and after learning she had cancer, Hubley made her first film by herself.

"Women of the World" presented a creative history of the earth through an animated collage of world art and from a feminist point of view.

"Women of the World" is in color and is 11 minutes long. Hubley's initial solo effort, released in 1975, went on to acceptance as an official entry at Cannes Film Festival and a CINE Golden Eagle.

"I was being given six months at a time," she said, "so if I was going to do something, it had to be done then. And after that, I did another one because I was still terminal." "Second Chance: Sea," 1976, also 11 minutes, is a look at the wonders of the world's oceans and a plea for international cooperation in preserving them. The film also won a CINE Golden Eagle and was featured at the Annecy Film Festival in France.

"I wasn't sure what I was doing, but I kept going," Hubley recalled.

The Hubley collaboration, who did what, could not be defined easily nor described, she said. They worked on the storyboard, a visual scenario, together. Then moved on to the sound and score. Her husband, she said, did most of the drawing, although she would draw her ideas. They designed the characters together and agreed on the layouts.

"John was the spokesman for our team and received director's credit," she said. "In return, he agreed to change his lifestyle and be home and have dinner with the children. He mellowed through time and I began to receive more credit. I feel it was a balanced collaboration. I know my vision is equally in the films."

Faith Hubley

The late Howard Weaver, dean of the art department at Yale, did a documentary, "In Quest of Cockaboody," about how the Hubleys worked. The big fight scene in it, Hubley recalled, was caused by a disagreement over a line of dialogue.

"But I don't believe there's anything wrong with fighting," she added. "Having the male and female input is very good."

Her husband, she said, could not face her illness. "Some men can, some men can't," she said. "It was interesting. What do you do if you have a problem? You run away.

"He went to London to direct a feature called 'Watership Down.' They offered him his name in lights and a lot of money. He was fired before the film was completed. It was very difficult for him and it was difficult for me."

Within six months, John Hubley was dead. "When you ask how did I live through it, I don't know. We did reconcile before he died. I was in and out of the hospital. No. I know how I did it. I had these four great kids."

At the time of John Hubley's death they had been working on "A Doonesbury Special." The half-hour special for NBC would feature Zonker Harris and his friends' responses to the changing values that marked the end of the 1960s.

When NBC questioned her ability to finish the production, Garry Trudeau, the creator of Doonesbury, went to bat for her and together they completed the film.

"A Doonesbury Special" collected an Academy Award nomination, a special jury prize at the Cannes Film Festival, and another CINE Golden Eagle.

After that, Hubley was free to create her own work. Her 17 prize-winning films include "Whither Weather," "Step by Step," "Sky Dance," "The Big Bang and Other Creation Myths," "Enter Life," "Starlore," "Hello," "The Cosmic Eye," "Time of the Angels," "Yes We Can," "Who Am I?," "Upside Down," and "Seers and Clowns."

How did she get through the next few years? "If you're in for the ride, you're in for the ride. I didn't have any system. I did Tai Chi. I had analysis. I have worked all my life. I love my life. The only things that were hard was his dying, being alone, and never having enough money."

Hubley described her children as self-supporting, happy, gifted, and good people. "They are a great source of pleasure to me," she said, "and for me, life's biggest reward." Her oldest son, married with two sons, is working toward a master's degree in preparation for a second career. Her second son is a film editor, married to a film editor. They live in New York with their daughter.

Hubley's daughter, Emily, is a filmmaker and mother of two. The youngest Hubley, a daughter, is a drummer. She and her husband have a band, "Yo La Tengo," write music, and are "very loved by their fans."

As far as Faith Hubley's life's work, that remains much as it's always been. She creates the film. She leaves the marketing to others.

Art comes from personal convictions and vision. John and Faith Hubley became a team because their beliefs and images were similar—"to increase awareness, to warn, to humanize, to elevate vision, to suggest goals, to deepen understanding of ourselves and our relationships to one another."[4]

Many of their films, and of hers, show the world through the eyes of children. "We wanted to say something about children, the world children deserve and need to live in," Hubley said. "Because we both had hard childhoods, we probably had more sensitivity and certainly had better eyes."

Hubley's days begin with music which has been an important facet of her life since childhood. She practices her cello then goes on to paint. Her afternoons are spent working on her current film. She gets up early and goes to bed early, except in the final stages of production when pressures for completion build.

On average, her films are ten minutes long. Only one, "The Cosmic Eye," (1985, silver medallion Houston Film Festival; USA Film Festival; Zagreb World Festival) was feature length. She didn't expect to do another of that length because of cost. "If I got other people's money and did one, it would have to make money. Then I'd have to do something I maybe wouldn't want to do."

Had being a woman in a male-dominated field held her back?

"Men get there quicker," she said. "I don't think a man would have got to where I am. I got where I got because I'm me." She wrote later, in respect to that question, "I don't see creativity as a race."

No, she said, being in her early 70s was not a problem, not in the least. "I love aging. I've never had more fun. My eyes have never twinkled this way."

And indeed, though twinkling eyes is a cliche straight out of a paperback novel of romance, when Hubley laughed, as she did so frequently, her eyes actually sparkled with light, underlining her thoughts in a rather mystical way.

"I understand life and death pretty well. I have no foolish expectations. I love the minute. I love the here and now. It's a glorious, beautiful world. I think we're going through shaking transitions, but I believe they are transitions. I'd like to be around to see how it comes out. I'm confident it's going to be OK. Most of our ancient religions and beliefs tell us that."

She's religious, but not in the sense of membership in an organized church. She called her beliefs in a higher power a patchwork quilt, composed of ideas and philosophies acquired along the way.

We left the studio and wound up business in the living room area.

The room appeared ordinary, somewhat dark in spite of windows with a river view; nothing fancy or dear, at least not obviously so. Steel shelves against a wall held rows of metal film canisters.

Opposite them, three Oscars lined up on a ledge. They weren't really a feature of the room. They had to be discovered.

Did she have plans for retirement? Perhaps a different way of life? Hubley shook her head: "I'll continue like I am," she said, "and then I'll die."

1 "Animated Women:" Patty Wineapple, producer; Sybil Del Guadio, director.
2 Films by John and Faith Hubley and by Faith Hubley are distributed in the USA by Lightyear Entertainment, 350 Fifth Avenue, Suite 5101, New York, N.Y. 10118, 1-800- 229-7867; and by Pyramid Film and Video, P.O. Box 1048, Santa Monica, California, 90406, 1-800-421-2304.
3 "Amazonia," 1989; distributed by Pyramid.
4 From The Films of John and Faith Hubley by Sybil DelGaudio.

2

Iona Hardy Campagnolo, born 1932, northern British Columbia; housewife, mother, until her mid-30s then reinvented her life to become Member of Parliament, first woman president Liberal Party; retired 1986 and kept going: university chancellor, TV panelist, women's and human rights activist.

For almost all of the time from the age of seven until I was seventeen, my home was a salmon cannery on the Skeena River near Prince Rupert...My father was the port engineer in charge of all the vessels during the summer; in the winter he was the watchman. Most of the workers came up only during fishing season in the summer, so my brother and I were pretty well the only kids year-round. It could get lonely.

"The cannery was rigidly class-divided—white collar workers, blue collar workers (which we were), Japanese and aboriginal people. We went to a one-room schoolhouse on the river and when we had our lunch hour, everyone would sit in their own little racial or social group...

"We had come from Galiano Island. I suppose, looking back, we were very poor, but Mother always had a way of making things comfortable...

"From 1942 until 1945, we lived in Vancouver during the winter and went north to the cannery by steamship in the spring. I remember everyone was in great fear that the Japanese submarines would come and attack us while we were journeying up the coast. The other years, we stayed north at the cannery all year around. [1]

"One day, in the spring of 1942, when I was nine years old, we all went down to the tracks to say goodbye to the Japanese who were being shipped to internment camps. The First Nation kids already had gone—to the distant, residential, government-run schools—when the naval ships came into the river to organize the removal of the Canadians of Japanese ancestry, eventually towing great flotillas of the Japanese fishing boats to a central location. But the people and only as many goods as they were able to carry, were removed by train. It is at the train tracks that my memory of their departure is seared in my mind. My brother and I were almost the only children left behind that spring, and we thought there was something wrong with us because we weren't being included in what we then thought were great adventures.

"I spent a lot of time on my own on the river... I used to read a great deal, an enormous amount of archeological, historical, and religious literature. I always thought I'd be a missionary of some kind. I never thought of becoming a minister, because I was a female.

"When I was eight, I was offered a job 'turning cans to the mountain' for labels. But I was too short to qualify. Two years later, I went back to work on the 'clincher' that put lids on the cans of salmon. But I was still too short so the China boss—a Chinese foreman of all the cannery's hourly workers who also punched our time cards—had a small platform built for me so I could reach the machine. Later as a teenager, I worked in the company store where people paid in scrip that was redeemed at the season's end by deducting from the total earned.

"In those days it was no disgrace to work at that age. There was no child labor law or anything like it, and occasionally we'd work 16 hours a day.

"At thirteen, I couldn't go to school at the cannery anymore because the river school ended at grade seven, so I started boarding in Prince Rupert. It was a very lonely time for me... I ended up with Miss Mary-Ann Way, a British spinster, as she called herself.

"(She) ran the literary club of Prince Rupert and taught music, and she really put me on the path to self-learning. Every night I was with her, she would play music, and I would read Shakespeare. She would make me read lines again and again until I was speaking them as beautifully as she could imagine. Because I was brought up with First Nation and Japanese children my diction was very poor. I softened the S's in the aboriginal style of speaking language other than English and occasionally left words out as the Japanese did.

"Later, speech teacher Will Hankinson and his Demosthenes Club polished what Miss Way had begun. My mother (had) despaired of us ever speaking English correctly. That I ended up in Parliament was a great shock to her on that ground alone."

That early history in a remote, wild and sparsely settled district on the Canadian-Alaskan border in no way suggested the poised and distinguished woman across the table. Certainly not her credentials:

- Member of Parliament for Skeena (94,000 residents scattered throughout an area the size of France), 1974-1979;
- Cabinet minister, fifth woman, 1976-1979;
- First woman president, Liberal Party, 1982-1986.

Iona Campagnolo had ridden a ferry from her island home to the city of Vancouver earlier in the day for an appointment with a wealthy businessman she hoped would endow a chair of ethics at the university of which she's chancellor. After the interview in her sister's apartment near the airport, she'd speak at an evening banquet.

I'd read of her in books and in newspaper clippings from her years in the public eye. Intriguing bits such as..."Campagnolo had both exceptional beauty and a toughness born out of fending for herself as a divorcee in a northern British Columbia town." [2]

Twenty years after that description of how she'd made it in the macho world of Canadian politics, Campagnolo hadn't a trace of toughness, but the beauty remained—classic features, high cheek bones and finely-textured skin. Her hair, brown and shoulder-length in early photos, had turned silver, was cut short and brushed away from her face. She wore a black turtleneck sweater, black slacks, black and green checked jacket, short and nipped in expensively in the right places.

Where had she picked up the confidence that took her from a kitchen and nursery in Prince Rupert, a remote town of about 15,000, to the halls of power in Ottawa? Miss Way, she said, had been an enormous influence in her life. Not just speech and music appreciation, but teaching her to look closely at all the options in a situation and then to make her decision based on reason.

"I was 33," Campagnolo said, "when I realized that I could apply these choices to my own life, that I was capable of doing many other things than society in the 1950s accorded women.

"In high school, I had been one of two top students—sometimes I was first, he was second, the next time the other way around. He went on to university and a Rhodes scholarship—he's now a lawyer in London. For me, university was a thousand miles away. The social pressure on women then was to marry and have babies. I have never regretted either, but it is a part of one's life, not the whole substance."

After graduating from high school, Campagnolo worked in a bank in Prince Rupert and then a utility company office. At 20, she married Louis Campagnolo, a fisherman. A year later, the first of their two daughters was born. She kept busy—taking night school courses, whatever was offered, volunteering for whatever good cause recruited her. She worked as advertising sales manager for a local radio station, found time to produce and direct musicals and plays with the little theater group, and was active in the garden club.

She'd not been bored by her life in Prince Rupert and never believed that being a woman limited her choices or lowered her status. "I didn't learn that until I got to Ottawa, and then it was too late..."

What launched Campagnolo's political career was a vice-presidency of the garden club.

"The president was Dutch and hadn't been in Canada very long so he spoke English with difficulty. When we opposed developers who wanted to take over the last main park in town, I spoke for the club.

"When we'd won the battle, local leaders said, 'You did such a good job beating city hall on the park, we want you to run for office.' They suggested alderman. I said to myself, 'AlderMAN? I don't think so.' They said 'What about school trustee?'" She won the contested seat by 21 votes and within a year became school board chair, winning subsequent elections overwhelmingly.

Why politics? "I felt I was, in spite of being involved in community affairs, operating at half speed. I believe most people go through life at half speed and I didn't want to.

"During the time I was in government, I worked at close to capacity. But I've always worked hard. I was brought up that way. My father believed in it and worked hard himself. I was taught, 'You have to walk what you talk.' I just thought, surely, I could be more valuable and when the opportunity arose to run for office I did so. That I was elected was a miracle of my time, or perhaps an accident, but I gave it all I had, nonetheless."

As frequently happened, chance determined fate. It was the manager of the radio station where she worked who wanted the Liberal Party candidacy for Member of Parliament for Skeena District. The plan was, he would run, Campagnolo would manage his campaign. but when the time for that came, a personal situation made his candidacy impossible. She ran. He worked back-stage, she recalled, wearing his best tie, inscribed "chauvinist pig" in tiny letters.

She looked back on the race as an introduction to her political career—high-energy and intense, grueling, exhausting, and a preview of the next dozen years: "Once I'm committed to something, it is in my nature to want to do it in the best way I can." She recalled her campaigns nationally on behalf of the Liberal Party: "St John's (Newfoundland) is a 4 1/2-hour time lag. I'd fly in late at night and have to be filled with energy and enthusiasm—and look decent—for a 7:30 party breakfast meeting. And be the same at the sixth event of the day—knowing there was another still ahead. Sometimes I'd calculate where my next sleep would be. One night might be in a suite in a four-star hotel, the next night in a dingy motel next to a fast food place. But I never paid any attention anyway, I'd just grope my way to the bed."

"I thought I had to do everything as quickly and hard as I could. I had to be able to say to myself, when it was over, 'I gave it my best.' And then, when it came to defeat, it was survivable."

Her political objectives never changed: "Everything I've done is based on combating the three 'isms'—racism, classism, and sexism. We've done well here on class I think. Racism is more subtle, a different set of problems in Canada. While whites in the U.S. killed off the aboriginal people, we moved them to reserves. I grew up with Indian kids and they're no different from me. The time has come to find a way to build their confidence.

"At UNBC (University of Northern British Columbia) we've got about a hundred Indian students—we call them the First Nation people now—and we hope to add many more in the years ahead. They, like I, were denied access in the past. But no more.

"As far as sexism, that's being mitigated under law. It's becoming a bit easier for us every year, I think. We're now seeing women pass through barriers, never knowing that barriers had been there."

Campagnolo and her husband separated when she entered politics: "A very reasonable separation. I thought it well done on both of our parts." No, she had not remarried, did not intend to. "I've become too independent."

When she entered Parliament in 1974, she became one of nine women members. She, like all but two of them—and most women politicians she would meet later—were either separated, divorced, or had never married. "That 'public women' have spouses now is an undiscussed but important leap forward to more normal lives for women in the public eye," she said.

"There are very few men who can stand the stress of a high-profile woman companion. There are very few men who would even date a female cabinet minister. When you go into a room, you just take all the oxygen out of it. You're the one everyone wants to talk to. Suddenly, at the end of the evening, you're looking around for your escort, to try to take the poor soul out the door with you. It's embarrassing; It's also what men have done to women since time immemorial, but a woman can't do it to them.[3] Surely if you felt warmly about a man, you would not subject him to that kind of discomfort. Feminism to me has never meant doing to men what they have done to us, but the opposite."

When Margaret Thatcher visited Canada just before becoming prime minister, Prime Minister Pierre Trudeau wanted to chat privately with her. He asked Campagnolo to engage her husband, Denis, in conversation. "I asked him what it was like to be the spouse of a very prominent woman. He told me, 'It's not so bad. What I do is provide her with diamonds, walk around at parties, and put a fresh glass in her hand when the one she's holding is warm...'"

After Campagnolo was elected to Parliament the first time, her only sister, Marion, 10 years younger, called: "'What are you going to do about Jennifer?' she asked me. My oldest daughter, Jan, was away from home by then, but Jennifer was a teenager. Mimi said 'I'll come to Ottawa with you. I'll take care of her.' She wasn't married then and she quit her job to do it. In addition to caring for Jennifer, she was my hostess and took my dry cleaning in, got my shoes to the repair shop. Public women are handicapped by not having 'wives' and I really could not have done it without her. I'll always be making up that debt to her."

After Trudeau named Campagnolo minister of state for fitness and amateur sport, a political columnist wrote: "She has courage, panache, vitality, virility, persuasiveness, directness, and a giant sense of commitment... (on) the other side, (she's) manipulative, superficial, stubborn, partisan and patronizing. Also she looks too good..." [4]

"It was a tiny little portfolio," she said of her cabinet appointment, "but I went back to the old actor's guide which says there are no small parts, only small actors." [5] Within a year, reporters were calling her one of Trudeau's most famous ministers.

Campagnolo's first defeat came in 1979, when she lost her bid for reelection by 269 votes. She attributed this to the Liberal government's ending subsidies to shipping in her district. Newspapers speculated that she would accept a cabinet position. She said she would not play an unelected role and didn't. She dropped out of sight, traveled to Thailand for volunteer work at a Canadian-run camp for Indo-Chinese refugees, then came home to start a public relations business and to appear in a CBC-TV show, "One of a Kind," until 1981.

"Political loss," she said, "is not like any other loss. When you lose politically, it is very public. It teaches you a good deal. In some ways, it is harder for a woman because there is a part of the public that would love to see you be frail or vulnerable or weep, but you mustn't do that. I had set up some psychological back-ups for myself in case I did lose, in that I had worked 100 percent... I came out of it relatively unscathed psychologically, but there is a great sense of loss.[6] It is a kind of death to be mourned and surmounted."

She added, "I didn't look in the mirror for weeks after the defeat and when I did, I didn't recognize myself.

Iona Hardy Campagnolo

"I was healthy. I looked rested. It was the first time I'd been rested in years."

In 1982, Trudeau's strategists urged her to run for Liberal Party president. The idea was not without opponents. "Members of my own party shoved misogynistic notes under my door during the party convention at which the vote took place," she said, "— objecting to my temerity, to putting myself up for an office traditionally held by men. And to make it even more controversial, no one had challenged an incumbent before."

Campagnolo campaigned for party leadership on a promise to wipe out the party's debt of nearly $2.6 million. She won by over a 2-1 margin. A year later, she announced a $100,000 surplus plus internal reform to democratize the party and take decision-making out of smoke-filled backrooms.

In 1983, political reporters spoke enthusiastically of Campagnolo as Liberal Party candidate for prime minister. She said she would not be a candidate. She repeated that, over and over.

"In power town, no one believed that anyone with a chance at the brass ring would avoid it," she said.

"I knew we were going to lose to the Conservatives in the next election. For me it would be a lose-lose situation. If, by some chance, I'd won, it would have been said it was because I was a woman that the party lost the government. If I lost, it would have been for the same reason.

"Also, I had only five years in politics and a minor portfolio at that. I hadn't had the proper education either. I've always felt the lack of a university education and for party leader, I think you need some Sorbonne under your belt, or to have been at Oxford, or a Rhodes scholar. A full, broad education at the highest levels of achievement is mandatory in my book."

If prime minister hadn't been her goal, what was it? "I'm not sure I ever put a cap on it. To keep fighting all these issues—racism, classism, sexism, human rights, democratic development—that regulate our behavior, and move toward finding whatever vehicle I could to help improve things."

She did stand again for Parliament in 1984, from a Vancouver district. "I did it to help represent (John) Turner, running for election as (Liberal Party) prime minister from Vancouver. It was of great significance to B.C. that a Liberal prime minister chose to run from our province. I traveled from one side of the country to the other, giving speeches and doing all-candidate forums for him when he couldn't."

From this time, another Campagnolo legend: "...Turner had gotten himself into a mess of his own...ignoring the pleas of his handlers to quit his disagreeable habit of slapping women on their derrieres, (Turner) had patronizingly patted the behind of two Liberal women in public.

"One of these happened to be party president Iona Campagnolo, who had not so good-naturedly returned the favor—five times—all in front of a CTV camera.[7]

"It trivialized my career," she said later. "But I knew he had no notion of it. It was locker-room behavior, as he would have treated a buddy."

Days before the election, a political columnist wrote she'd "earned her opponent's ungrudging respect for a gritty, sparkling campaign...a star candidate...chief party spokesman ...tireless door knocker...a poised, confident performance...but it is likely Campagnolo will join Turner and 26 other British Columbia Liberals in defeat..." As it turned out, Turner was the only Liberal elected in British Columbia. Said a senior New Democrat party organizer, "If there were any justice, she would be the one Liberal here to survive the debacle." A political writer said "the rap against her is that she is not a complete team player." And a senior Liberal said "Iona is a bit of an eccentric person. She has her own agenda and her own ideas."[8]

Campagnolo said, "I always felt they would have preferred me as their malleable mouthpiece. They found it difficult to accept that I had my own ideas. My place was outside the circle...I'm not part of the gang and I never will be. It has to do with being born an 'Outer British Columbian' as well as being female in a male time."

Though she lost in the Liberal rout, that same year, party members reelected her to a second two-year term as the party president.

In 1986 she said she would not seek a third term and she did not. "I've watched others stay too long at the fair. I was determined to step off the stage in 1986 on my own initiative and I really did. I worked in West Africa for a bit, legally resumed my maiden name for private life, but this name is who I have become and it's a good Canadian name. I don't think I suffered any withdrawal. I knew intimately what the job was. And the price. I wasn't damaged by the experience; to the contrary, I now think I was enriched by it."

In one of her final interviews, she said, "A lot of people think what I do is glamorous and to some degree, I like to make it seem that way, even though half the time I'm dead tired and deeply fatigued and sometimes depressed like anyone else, (but) I will go to some length to make sure it is fun for those who are watching..." [9]

Though politics sounded like a grueling and exhausting job with few visible satisfactions, Campagnolo believed the rewards worth the price: "I have the knowledge of how the system works and I know this country from one end to the other. I've been in just about every city, town and hamlet in Canada. I can knock on a door—any door—and as soon as it opens, tell you about the people who live in the house.

"And I know who to call. All of this is a wonderful satisfaction. I'm good at bringing diverse interests together. Just before I came today, my agent called to tell me I'll be moderating this huge salmon conference. I could never have done that before—bring all those deeply vested interests together—but I can now. I've become a good synthesizer and that's a useful skill.

"I keep urging young women to write our history—to give us chronicles of our past that don't yet really exist. I think every woman in my generation felt she was her own creation. In my early thirties, I really believed I was just coming into my own as a person, that I was more than an extension of my husband or children or community.

"I advise every young woman to consider all the phases of her personality. I was a pretty girl in my town. After high school, Jantzen offered me a contract to model swimsuits. I turned it down because I always knew pretty girls didn't last long. But a job like that was a way out of the north—like the boy who followed the hockey puck out of town. In some ways, though, I never really left. I've worked for my community in various ways, up to the present day. Because of UNBC, for instance, Northerners will no longer be denied access to the very best post-secondary education. In our first year of operations, the percentage of Northerners entering university has doubled."

As for Campagnolo's goals now, "There are no great mountains I want to climb."

A few years earlier, she'd bought a small house in a valley on Vancouver Island. Again that summer, she'd move, by wheelbarrow load, her annual spring delivery of 10 yards of soil for the garden she'd been developing. She enjoyed her role as grandmother of three.

"I rather think that should I have enough money to do so," she said, "I will audit philosophy courses in my old age—fast approaching.

"It's interesting that my life as an adult, like my childhood, was very often taken up with living in two places, one rural, one city, and continues in that mode. Frankly, I do not feel at all rooted unless I spend at least part of my time in B.C. We are fourth generation there, with a great-grandfather, Findlay Murcheson, who established residence on Galiano Island in 1882, and was among the first non-aboriginals to do so."

In 1992, Campagnolo was named chancellor of Canada's newest university, the University of Northern British Columbia, officially opened by Queen Elizabeth II in 1994. Its main campus is in Prince George, but it is linked electronically with the entire, vast region. She's a regular panelist on World Affairs for PBS in the United States. She's on a dozen Canadian boards and committees, everything from the Centre for Sustainable Regional Development to the Canadian Native Arts Foundation and the Osteoporosis Society.

"In 1986," Campagnolo said, "I decided I would devote half of my time to making enough money to live on. The other half I would give away." She has no pension.

At the end of our interview her sister, Marion, whom she called Mimi, arrived. She'd been helping her husband stack boxes of fish at the market they owned. There was an easiness between the sisters and an obvious affection. Papers were organized, coats collected, and goodbyes said.

In the days that followed, I thought a great deal about the amazing Iona Campagnolo. Truly amazing. A focused, extremely well-informed woman of enormous energy, honesty—what you see is what you get—exceptional wit, intelligence, close ties with her family. But still this nagging sense of having missed an essential part of her. Much later, reading through newspaper clippings, there it was: "At her center, Iona Campagnolo is a cool, detached, efficient human being whose passions are absorbed in ideas." [10]

In a letter, Campagnolo explained, "I am convinced that ideas are the only hard currency of our time.

"I will receive my first honorary degree (this spring) from Simon Fraser," the letter continued. "I guess that might indicate I am no longer considered a dangerous women. As for eccentric, well, that is one of the nicer things I have heard said about me...

"Most often, I have simply been thought of as an alien presence in traditional male preserves.

"My life choices have just been different than the majority society. That doesn't make them wrong, perhaps just not in fashion in my time.

"I have been very often accepted, welcomed, even while being considered sometimes a threat to the established order. It seems reasonable to me that should be so, in the circumstances."

1 Taped by Sid Tafler for Today magazine, July 10, 1981.
2 From *Grits, An Intimate Portrait of the Liberal Party,* by Christina McCall-Newman; 1982; page 378.
3 *Gilded Ghetto, Women and Political Power in Canada,* by Sydney Sharpe; Harper Collins Ltd.; 1994.
4 Homemakers magazine, by Even Rockett, September 1977.
5 "Gilded Ghetto..."
6 The Sunday Sun, Sutton's People, February 6, 1983.
7 *Mulroney: The Politics of Ambition,* by John Sawatsky; 1971; page 534.
8 Dan Smith in the Toronto Star; September 7, 1984.
9 Hubert Bauch in the Toronto Star; September 29, 1984.
10 Carol Goar in the Toronto Star; November 1, 1986.

3

Anne Wexler, CEO The Wexler Group, lob-
byists, consultants; born 1930; B.A., LLD
(honorary) Skidmore; doctor of science (honorary) Bryant College; associate publisher Rolling Stone; assistant to President Carter; director Dreyfus, New England Electric System,
Alumay, Comcast Corp., Nova Corp; board
memberships include Washington Economic
Club, National Park Foundation.

Other than her decision to leave politics—that brief stint at
Rolling Stone magazine in the mid-1970s—Anne Wexler
believed the events which moved her to high places were
"pretty serendipitous. I could hardly say I'd planned it. In 1970, I
was a housewife running a political campaign. In 1978, I worked
in the White House."

We talked in the offices of the Washington, D.C., firm Wexler
founded in January 1981.

Looking back to determine what early influences helped her
to make that transition from homemaker to White House staffer,
she said: "I think the strongest influence as I matured was my experience in college. I'm a very strong advocate of women's colleges. Skidmore is now coed, but at that time it was a women's

school. I particularly remember being nurtured through four years of history by two fabulous professors, both women.

"When you think about it, women's schools like Skidmore, Wellesley and Smith, were, in many ways, a kind of substitute for affirmative action. They provided—without anyone ever thinking about it—an atmosphere where you didn't have to worry about, essentially, being a second class anything. This was in the late '40s and early '50s: The professor didn't call on the male in our classes and, at that time, there was interest in doing that.

"We came out of women's institutions with a strong conviction about our own skills and our own abilities—without any equivocation—into a world which certainly didn't expect us to be that way. That was the most impressionable period of my life and I think college gave me a lot of confidence which I probably wouldn't otherwise have had."

Anne Wexler was born in 1930 in New York City. The family—she has a brother eight years younger—moved to Newport News, Virginia, when she was 12 years old, after her father entered the military during World War II. She split her high school years between there and Connecticut. By profession, her father was an architect. Her mother, a paid Red Cross worker during the war years, did volunteer service before and after that time.

In retrospect, she saw her interest in politics and government as a natural extension of around-the-family-dinner-table political discussions when she was growing up. Books also proved an influence.

"I was a voracious reader," Wexler recalled. "Everything and anything." She worked her way from adventure tales to chronicles of America's social history by such writers as John Dos Passos, Theodore Dreiser, and Sinclair Lewis. Part of her interest in books may have been because of a period of family transiency.

"Until I became socialized and adjusted," Wexler said, "My response was to read. I still read a lot—biography, history, archaeology." At that time, she was reading Roger Kennedy's "Hidden Cities" on the ancient Native American mound cultures in the southern part of the country, and a biography of President Bill Clinton by David Maraniss in which, she added, both she and her husband, Joe Duffey, figured prominently. When Clinton was a Yale law student, he worked for Wexler in the Duffey for Senate campaign.

During her high school and college years, she gave little thought to her future. "I graduated from Skidmore College in 1951. Most of the women in my class were pretty preoccupied with getting married. I became engaged my senior year and married about a month after I graduated. I did go right to work, though—at a radio station, basically writing press releases. A year later I shifted to an advertising agency where I stayed until my husband entered the Air Force in 1953. He was stationed at Geneva, New York, and when we moved there, I stopped working. I had my first child in 1954. We went back to New York in 1956, when my second son was born, and in 1958, we moved to Connecticut."

She and her husband divorced in the mid-1960s.

In Connecticut, Wexler stepped up her political activities. Earlier, she'd done mailings, putting on stamps and sealing envelopes, for Adlai Stevenson's 1952 and 1956 campaigns. And with Wexler, Stevenson still ranked the highest among the country's top political figures.

In Connecticut in the 1960s, she moved from political involvement at the local level to district then to state campaigns. In 1964, she'd worked for Lyndon Johnson's candidacy.

Disillusioned with escalation of the Vietnam War, she became involved with the anti-war movement. She organized a campaign for an anti-war slate of convention delegates from her congressional district in 1966. Though these delegates were seated, the candidate they backed lost. However, Wexler's reputation as a skillful campaign organizer became apparent and in 1967 she was approached by those running Eugene McCarthy's campaign.

At that time, she met Joe Duffey, now her husband. "Joe and I co-chaired the McCarthy campaign in Connecticut in 1968, and we both went to Chicago as delegates. We ran primaries in every town in the state—a big effort and very successful—and that, essentially, was what moved me from the state to the national level."

Two years later, she became campaign manager of Duffey's bid for a Senate seat.

Though he lost, she gained fame as the only woman in the United States that year to run a Senate campaign.

After teaching at the Kennedy School of Government at Harvard, Wexler returned to Washington, D.C. in 1974 to join Rolling Stone magazine. That marked a major change in career goals, a decision based on what must have been a painful conclusion: She could not earn a living in politics.

"A friend at Rolling Stone, Richard Goodwin, had asked me if I would come and work with him and, at that time, the magazine was deeply involved in a lot of political coverage," she said. "I worked closely with many of the writers, helping promote that side of the magazine. But I got interested in the business end and shortly was asked to be associate publisher and work on, essentially, business things, such as circulation and promotion. During that time, we started a Rolling Stone news service and a lecture bureau, and I stayed on through the 1976 presidential campaign.

"I'd met Jimmy Carter in 1974 when he was chairing the Democratic National Party's congressional campaign committee, now defunct. He'd gone to Bob Strauss, chairman of the Democratic National Committee, and asked if he could chair that committee. Carter was then ending his term as governor of Georgia.

"The idea was to travel throughout the country in support of Democratic congressional candidates. This gave him entree to many places and a chance to work with many candidates.

"Strauss asked me to be on that committee so I worked with Carter in 1974. The staff director of the committee was Hamilton Jordan who went on to be Carter's campaign manager and eventually his chief of staff. So, when Carter was elected, Hamilton called and asked if I would be a member of the transition team. He put together a small group—I believe about eight or ten—to work directly with him and oversee the transitions in each of the cabinet departments. He asked my husband to oversee the HHS transition—Health and Human Services, then called Health, Education and Welfare. He asked me to do the same with the Department of Commerce. Both of us left our jobs—at that time, my husband was chief executive officer of the AAUP, American Association of University Professors.

"We went in with the transition and after the inauguration, I became deputy undersecretary of Commerce and Joe became secretary of state for Education and Cultural affairs."

About a year later, President Carter invited Wexler to come to the White House as his Assistant for Public Liaison. At about that same time, he named Duffey chairman of the National Endowment for the Humanities.

Wexler remained in her key position at the White House until early 1981 when she founded The Wexler Group.

"I had a choice," she explained. "I could either go to work for a corporation doing some of the same things I'd done in the White House or start my own firm.

"I basically decided it would be more fun to work for myself than for someone else, and would have more potential and opportunity as well."

Wexler's office was spacious, but welcomingly informal, with a couch against the wall opposite and an oversize desk in a multiwindowed alcove at the other end of the room. Wexler looked smart: flame-red tailored suit with a slubby surface, waist-length jacket, knee-length skirt, understated gold jewelry. Tanned and handsome, her well-modulated voice was reassuring—everything was on the right track.

After she began her own business, she continued, Duffey stayed on as chairman of NEH, this being a term rather than a political appointment, for another year—during the Reagan administration. A few months later, early in 1982, he was named president of the University of Massachusetts and moved to Amherst.

Wexler and Duffey arrived at what seemed a characteristically unique answer to jobs in different cities. "I had just started this business so we made an arrangement," she said. "Essentially, it was that we would commit to being together every weekend. And we missed only one in nine years—when I was traveling with Geraldine Ferraro (Democratic vice-presidential candidate) on the West Coast during the 1984 campaign.

"Clients would call and say, 'We'd like to have you speak at our convention in Palm Beach on Saturday.' And I'd say, 'I'm sorry, I don't do weekends.'

"You have to make a rule and stick to it. We'd also decided that to the degree that we could possibly organize it, we wouldn't work on weekends. We had a great time. I was out of here around noon on Fridays, flew to Hartford where a university driver picked me up. There was a phone in the car, and I got a lot of business done on the drive to Amherst.

"We had a wonderful housekeeper who did all the shopping and the cooking. I'd just show up. I didn't have to do any work and there was always lots of food in the refrigerator. It was like going to your country home for the weekend."

Two of their sons—like Wexler, Duffey has two sons—moved into the chancellor's Amherst house: one completed studies for an undergraduate degree, the other earned a Ph.D. during that time. One of her sons came to live in her Washington, D.C. apartment so both she and her husband had companionship. Looking back, she believed, in the main, their arrangement worked well, though both Duffey and she were ready for the next change: "After nine years of schlepping back and forth—two wardrobes, two everything—it got a little tired so in 1991, when Joe was asked to be president of American University here, we both moved into the president's house. Then two years later, Bill Clinton got elected and asked him to be director of the United States Information Agency and he left American University. And that's the way it will be, certainly, for the next two years. "After that, we'll see."

Anne Wexler

Looking back, Wexler saw the move from the Commerce Department to the White House as a major career step forward.

"Coming in a year later was not as easy as being there from the beginning, but I think I was able to organize that operation pretty well and over the years I've gotten a lot of praise for it. And it certainly helped launch this business.

"The truth of the matter is, anyone who has the opportunity to work for a President of the United States—well, it's got to be a unique and fabulous experience. I used to think to myself as I walked through those gates every day, just how special it was to do that."

When Wexler joined the White House team, she became the only woman on the senior staff. Much of her job at that level, she explained, "was firefighting. There are so many things to deal with on a minute-by-minute, hour-by-hour basis, you have to struggle for the time to do long-range planning—and it's important that you do that. We had all kinds of interesting challenges in the Carter

White House: dealing first of all with the energy crisis, then with inflation, and, of course, at the end, with the hostage crisis.

"My responsibility was essentially building public support for the President's priority issues. I was always dealing with contentious constituencies and, at the same time, trying to build enough public enthusiasm to make it easier for the President to deal with the Hill.

"It was a fascinating job and it required a lot of coordination with other departments in the White House.

"More than anything else, I think what I learned in the White House were the skills required to create teams of people who could work together to solve a problem and the importance of that. Essentially, that's what we do here. Everything's teamwork."

Basically, she said, The Wexler Group of which she is chairman and principal officer, engages in strategic planning, lobbying, coalition-building, grass-roots organizing around issues.

"In short, I guess you could say we manage issues as opposed to managing candidates—though a lot of what we do is political. We're bipartisan and everyone who works here—45 employees, 25 of them professionals—has served in the government."

That background is vital, she said. Knowledge of the way government works enables the firm to help clients make their way through the maze of details and potential roadblocks that surface hour by hour in dealings with government.

Wexler employees, half of them women, included a former Washington counsel for the American Medical Association; former members of the Clinton/Gore campaign's health care advisory group; several members of President Reagan's staff; a longtime staffer with the House Appropriations Committee; key campaigners for Bush/Quayle; a political cartoonist; and public relations person for a Robert Dole Senate campaign. Wexler Group clients include important trade associations as well as such varied giants of American business as General Motors, American Airlines, and Johnson and Johnson. At the time we talked, a significant recent victory had been direction of the 4,000-member coalition for USA

NAFTA (North American Free Trade Agreement). She'd followed that with the GATT (General Agreement on Trades and Tariffs) coalition and another win.

Her success, she said, lies in experience, managerial and organizational abilities and, "clearly," having a sensitivity to the differences between the way government functions and the way other institutions work. Decisions in the Wexler firm are essentially reached through consensus and compromise, by working through divisive issues. That horizontal structure is the essence of government, Wexler said, as compared to the vertical organization of the private sector where decisions come from the top down.

"The essential qualities of our business are service, quality and integrity," she said. "You have to understand how to deal with clients in terms of advising them and that includes telling them when they're wrong. Quality is really vital. Clearly as important in Washington is integrity—the understanding that you will always deal on an open and honest basis, not ever trimming or exaggerating.

"The other thing about us is we tend to be pretty selective about whom we represent. For instance, we would not represent a tobacco company nor would we ever work for an issue that was in any way inimical to women. If we don't agree on the position a client wants to take, we simply don't work for them. We're careful about conflicts, too. We do a lot of work in the trade area and have always been on the open market/free trade side. We don't turn around and work on a protectionist issue. For many years we've been involved in the cable industry. On that basis, it would be very hard for us to work for broadcasters.

"I think it is terribly important that even as personnel changes on (Capitol) Hill, people understand who you are, your reputation, and then you make sure you maintain that reputation. Pick a side and stay there."

Wexler's day usually began at 6 a.m. with 30 minutes on an exercise cycle: at work, meetings all day long and on the rare occasion there weren't meetings, sessions with staff or study on related matters. She and Duffey tried to keep weekends free for skiing in season, close friends, their sons, and two grandchildren. Twice a year, they scheduled a holiday away: Spain or Mexico for a couple of weeks in summer, family skiing holidays in Colorado during the winter.

She brought a photo from a nearby table, taken a few weeks earlier: a family line-up of handsome, smiling people in ski wear, arms around skis, against a background of snow and mountains.

"My husband and I like to walk," Wexler continued. "We go to the theater often. We like opera, the symphony. We have a busy social life and a lot of official stuff too, since he's head of an agency—though not as much as when he was university president."

As far as the future, Wexler said she doesn't make long range plans, prefers to let events unroll.

"I could never completely retire," she said, "but I hope to have a little more time—some time."

She'd considered the possibility of organizing her professional responsibilities in the future so she'd have a space of a month or more free rather than establishing a year when she'd stop working. A retirement home in Colorado appealed to her. Another possibility would be Florida where they own property.

"It's important, I think, to reinvent yourself," Wexler continued. "I'm looking forward to the next stage and I'm sure I'll find interesting things to do. When people do retire, I think it's good to get away, not stay if you're not a part of it. I see a good many people here who are angry because they're not involved."

During a brief break, there was time to look again at her office. A sense of a place where important matters were dealt with came through, along with the personality of the incumbent: thick carpeting, natural light; many paintings; tons of photos including many of Wexler and international superstars; editorial page cartoons, including a great many Oliphant cats, likely original, by famous cartoonists at major newspapers.

Among the photos was a younger Wexler and Duffey sitting on a park bench, oblivious of anything or anyone but each other.

On the lower border of a large, impressionistic watercolor of the White House, was written 'With gratitude for your contribution to the nation...Jimmy and Rosalynn Carter.'

Words by Camus had been done in calligraphy:

> *In the midst of winter*
> *I finally learned*
> *There was in me*
> *An invincible summer.*

We walked together to the outer office. Her building, Wexler said, was 110 years old and on the national register of historic buildings. The Wexler Group had occupied upper floor suites since 1983. The rooms were handsome indeed with lavish moldings and woodwork of dark oak, and crystal chandeliers suspended from tall ceilings.

In a less busy future, she said, in an abrupt change of subject, she'd perhaps own a dog. "I love dogs," she said, "but there's no hope for that now. Not with life as it is."

But, she continued, "I love this work, and it's always interesting. You're involved with different issues. There's always a challenge. It's learning something new all the time, mastering new things. It's working with people, both internally and externally, at all different levels: at the policy level, strategy level, implementation level. And it's fun, too. I honestly can't think of anything about this job I don't like."

4

Violet Anderson Hilbert, Native American;
born 1918; picked fruit, welded, ran a cafe,
and owned a beauty shop until 1972 when she
began teaching Skagit language and culture at
University of Washington. Since retiring,
she'd dedicated herself to preserving her heritage in books, texts, theater, and storytelling.
For her contributions, Seattle University
awarded her an honorary doctorate.

On the wall of the small frame house in Seattle hung a docu-
ment: Violet Hilbert, master artist; National Heritage Fellowship, September 1994; Folk and Traditional Arts Program, National Endowment for the Arts.

The award recognized that what Vi Hilbert did, no one else
had done. She found a way to put the Skagit culture and its
Lushootseed language of her childhood into words that others—
both her own and white people—could understand. This hadn't
been just a nice hobby for her spare time, but a life-driving force
that consumed her total attention.

Hilbert's modest one-story home faced a busy street and
looked over a steep bank that ended alongside the Duwamish River.
This was her house, where she'd lived since 1960 with Don, the

58

sailor she'd met in World War II, and their son and daughter, now adults with children and grandchildren of their own.

She first saw the land when she rode by in a bus, on her way to work. That place spoke to her, she said. Later she learned why. According to a legend of the Duwamish tribe, a battle between Northwind and Southwind occurred just about where Hilbert's house would be built, thus establishing it as the center of their world. What was visible these days, was urban industrial sprawl, split by freeways and a vast airfield owned by Boeing.

The main rooms of the house spilled into one another. They overflowed with boxes; baskets; rugs on chairs, tables and floor; video tapes; books; family photos, framed and unframed; arresting, poster-sized portraits of Native American elders, of canoes and paddlers, fog-shrouded rocky coastlines; stacks of papers; files; and piles of newspapers.

Somewhere among the books must have been some of her own. Hilbert co-authored Lushootseed language textbooks and two volumes of its literature plus a dictionary.

There is, among linguists, historians and anthropologists, increasing concern in preserving languages of Native Americans. As one said, "Tribes were created in language." Yet federal policy forbade the use of any such language from 1886 until the Native Americans Languages Act passed in 1990. Furthermore, when Native Americans were moved onto reservations, little attention was paid to the mix that would live together. As an expert put it, Native American languages are in great trouble.

When I met with Hilbert, she was deeply involved in balancing research to wind up her two volumes of tribal stories and history—revealed by elders on first-generation tape recorders—with speaking engagements on such topics as "Cultural Pluralism," and development of theater in Lushootseed. For the latter, she planned to dramatize tribal legends using a participatory audience and sophisticated recording methods, the videos to be sold to schools, libraries, and museums.

The tapes would be expensive, but necessarily so. Hilbert needed money to support her work. The $10,000 which came with her National Endowment of the Arts award helped. Though friends urge her to apply for grants, she refuses. Accept a grant, she said, and lose your soul.

The books particularly worried her. These must be done quickly, she said: "I'll be 77 this July (1995) and don't have time to mess around. I don't plan to become senile, but then, no one ever does. While my faculties are on the level, I need to get all of these things done. I have an agenda."

Her agenda developed late in life. This sense of mission—to speak of truths learned in childhood—didn't come to her until after a near fatal brain aneurysm in 1970.

"The illness made me focus on what was important," she said. "I had no time to waste. I'd been bending hair 10, 12, 14 hours a day to provide a living. I was quite artistic and I had many customers.

"My shop was right here"—she waved her arm in the direction of the kitchen—"in the south wing of the house, now the brain room where I do my research."

In "Writings about Vi Hilbert by her Friends," (edited by Janet Yoder), her husband wrote that after her illness she became a different person. "She changed a whole lot. She was afraid to leave the house for three or four months. It took a year to get her to drive again. This language deal filled in. She had delved a bit into art beadwork and making apple dolls before that. After the aneurysm, she totally lost interest in that and turned her attention to the culture. We still have her beadwork downstairs. She'd never looked at it since. Vi lost interest in the beach property. There was no more going out to camp every weekend. She also lost interest in square dancing."

When Hilbert could function again, she turned her attention to the past: "I went out in the field, talked to people I knew were fragile, began tape recording the elders who carry our history in their minds because it is their responsibility. Shortly after that I met Thom Hess for the second time."

A linguist, Dr. Hess had been invited by Indian Studies, as it was then called at the University of Washington, to offer a Salish language course. Hilbert signed up.

The 36 different tribes in the Pacific Northwest speak 20 different languages, many of them, like Lushootseed, in the Salish family and, to a degree, mutually understandable. Of the 550 Skagits, only a few could speak or understand Lushootseed. It was Hess who taught Hilbert a system for spelling her ancient language which had a symbol for every sound.

When the second term came round, Hess had only a day a week free to teach. He suggested to the university that Hilbert take over his language class. The university was easier to convince than Hilbert who still struggled with the effects of her illness—one of these being a tendency to weep when she spoke publicly in Lushootseed. Another being the awareness that she'd earned none of the scholastic credentials possessed by her colleagues. Eventually, she did consent and ended up directing a language and literature program that continued to grow until her retirement in 1989. Retirement for Hilbert did not mean leisure.

To understand Violet Anderson Hilbert, one must know of her early years, which were about as far from a middle-class Anglo girlhood of the time as it's possible to get, principally in community and parental expectations. No going to college, meeting a suitable boy and settling down to raise a family for her. To begin with she was the only survivor of Charley and Louise's eight children.

"I was taken everywhere," she recalled. "I was never left at home. While other children played outside, I had to sit beside my parents and listen to everything. My parents expected me to conduct myself properly so as never to disgrace my family or my people.

"I was never to speak at these occasions. Oh, I wanted to be like other children, but I was obedient and that was my responsibility to my parents.

"I don't think my parents knew exactly what I would do when I grew up, only that I would have work I would need to do and they must prepare me for leadership. In their wisdom they knew the oral tradition was how we lived and if I had this indoctrination, it would be everything I needed. I would know the rules of their world and I would abide by them. This would be my protection. My father said I would have spiritual help from our ancestors and this surrounds me. I have all the tools."

Hilbert's father, like many Native American males in the Pacific Northwest, worked as a logger to support his family. They went with him wherever the jobs were, her mother making a home for them in whatever this might be, sometimes a chicken house, other times a garage.

"Every winter," she said, "my mother loaded our Model-T with sleeping and eating necessities and we'd head for a longhouse/smokehouse gathering at Lummi or Swinomish or Tulalip. Indians from all over spent hours, days and nights, singing, dancing, listening, sleeping, and talking—maintaining and sharing the teachings. The foundations of my parents' life were the smokehouse culture and the Shaker Church. I fell asleep many, many nights under some bench in a Shaker church with the floor swaying to the movement of many pairs of feet and to the sound of dozens of bells."

Hilbert pondered the differences between organized Western religions and the beliefs of her people.

"Well, ours is not Christian, not gendered. It stems from spirituality, from a primary being, the focus—a sacred supernatural spirit our people have known since we were given life. Some of our people have earned the special gift which gives them strength to transcend these barriers (between earth and spirit world) to speak with the spirit. Its presence is always with us though it has no form. We trust this spirit implicitly and unconditionally to fulfill our reason for being here because this is the spirit that gave us life."

Violet Anderson Hilbert

While Christians believe in heaven, Native Americans she said "possess a comfortable knowledge that all of us depart with this spirit to join the souls on the other side."

Where is this other side? Hilbert grinned: "Beats me, but it's comforting to know there is such a place."

Like many of us, Hilbert holds a childhood incident as a talisman for adult life. "Because of my father's work, I was in and out of 15 schools before high school. In many I was the only Indian child. Of course, children love to pick on a cry baby and I was. When I was teased and picked on, I would bawl. If I went home bawling, my mother, after questioning me, would march to my school and raise Cain with the teacher. That, of course, only made things worse for me, so I learned to stop bawling before I got home.

"But one day had been especially bad. My dad was home and he could see I'd been crying. He asked what was the matter: 'The kids at school are so mean to me,' I told him. 'They called me all kinds of names and they pick on me all the time.' My father lifted me up, held me next to his face: 'I don't want to ever hear you feeling bad about something like this again. If I hear it, I'm going to put you in a gunny sack and nail you on the wall. You will stay in that sack and think about how foolish it is to allow ignorant people to make you feel sad. Those kids have not been taught how to be human beings. You have.' I never forgot that and since then I've never allowed ignorant people to make me angry.

"When I look at the Skagit girls of this generation, I feel very discouraged. The boob tube in the middle of the house, the welfare system. These things pulled the rug from under my people. That's why I am so anxious for Lushootseed literature to come out. I want to put one of my books in each (Skagit) village so an elder can read what has been left to them. This is my final work and my hope."

At Hilbert's 75th birthday party, people from both the Anglo and Native American communities came to honor her, including the governor of Washington, Mike Lowry. Skagits stood up to speak positively of her efforts, though not all approve.

"Some say you don't give white people anything," she explained. "They've robbed us of our culture and stolen our land. My answer to that is, the land, as we know it, is ours. No one can take it. Besides, if something truly belongs to you, no one can steal it."

Though Hilbert grew up with few material comforts, lost a first-born son at age three and a half from tubercular meningitis, and supported herself through hard work for many years, she considered herself fortunate—"extremely so."

She said, "I never thought of myself as being poor as a child—or after. I've chosen the way I want to live and I live in that fashion. I know I can do anything I choose to do. That belief has never been shaken. I don't allow it. That is the bottom line.

"I've accomplished what I have because people pushed me and then stood behind me. I couldn't let people down who believed in me. When they asked me to do things I didn't believe I could, I'd think, 'I don't have the intelligence to do these things. But I can't let them down by not trying.'

"I've often been urged to get the degrees those in academia think important. No. I don't need these. I have an education. Degrees are important in Thom's (Dr. Hess) world but not in mine. I'm an old grandmother—no, a great-grandmother—preserving the language and culture of my people. I'm not a linguist. I tell him, 'I can't learn to be tall,' but I don't think he understands.

"My adopted sister, who teaches at the University of Virginia, asked me to speak to her class about choosing career directions. I told them, 'Do each thing as that door opens. Fill your life with experiences. Don't feel like failures if you learn something that doesn't seem to fit. On this road, one career prepares you for another and you can have ten to get to the one you'll choose.'"

Hilbert suffered a second, though less serious, brain aneurysm about 10 years after the first. "This only strengthened my resolve to get my work done," she said. "I hadn't become a turnip, I'd been given another chance. How many times do you get another chance? If you don't hurry up, one of these things is going to get you."

5

Katherine Woodruff Fanning, editor, Christian
Science Monitor, Anchorage Daily News;
journalism educator; born 1927; Smith Col-
lege graduate; honorary degrees from Smith,
Harvard, and others; first woman president
American Society of Newspaper Editors.

Katherine Woodruff Fanning and her husband, Mo Mathews,
lived in an upper-floor condominium on Beacon Street in
Boston. In addition to an excellent address, their residence
came with choice views of boats on the Charles River and bicy-
clers, walkers, and runners on the paths along its banks.

On the walls throughout the many rooms of their home hung
photographs—many of them taken by Fanning—that documented
places and times in the years after she left Chicago and the life of
a wealthy society matron with the best name in town—Mrs.
Marshall Field, Jr.

The photographs included a fjord in China; a pre-election
meeting of KwaZululand voters in South Africa; buildings in
Prague; a Thailand waterway; southern African wildlife; a boat in
Kashmir; Russian rooftops; and a Scottish landscape. In another,
she hiked a trail hugging a vertical mountainside in Switzerland.

We settled into chairs around a table in a dining area open to
a large living room filled with fine, Far Eastern furniture, rugs,

and accessories. Fanning, tall and erect, moved energetically and spoke with certainty. She'd recently returned from Dallas, Washington, D.C., Chicago, New York, and points in California. That day she'd been winding up paperwork in the lower floor condominium she used as an office and packing for a month in Vietnam. Usually she traveled in connection with philanthropic and journalism-connected boards and societies. The trip coming up was, perhaps, a sentimental return to a land where 30 years ago, her engineer husband built roads.

Katherine Woodruff was born and grew up in Joliet, Illinois. "I was an only child," she said. "I came east to Westover School when I was about 14, then went on to Smith College. Somewhere along the line, I discovered I liked to write. At Smith, I took every writing course they had. I wrote plays, radio scripts, and short stories. I earned a bachelor's degree in 1949 and a year later, did what most young ladies of my age, in that era, did: I got married and had three children. My husband did not take to the idea of my working at all, but I did a lot of things as a volunteer—charity work, quote, unquote."

Marshall Field, Jr. was editor and publisher of the Chicago Sun-Times and during their marriage, acquired the Chicago Daily News.

No, she didn't learn journalism from him she said, but "he brought his problems at the office home and talked with me about them. I became very involved and I loved it."

After her divorce from Field in 1963 and during the emotional turmoils that followed, she'd sought a "much different, more down to earth, and simpler lifestyle." She moved from Chicago's Gold Coast to Old Town, resigned from Junior League, joined a Great Books group, and became active in the civil rights movement. Battling suicidal depression in the early months, she found a lifeline in the Christian Science religion, "the only thing that made sense to me, that made sense of the world, and of life."

A little over a year later, in 1965, she, her two pre-teen daughters, and son drove to Alaska. A close college friend lived in Anchorage. Fanning's plan was to stay a year, but she remained for 18 years.

"What I loved most about Alaska," she wrote in *New Guardians of the Press,* [1] besides the glory of its mountains and the glittering winter snow, was the warmth of its people. In Alaska, no one seemed to care who you had been or what you had done before you migrated north. Total equality. A classless society. A chance to begin again. I liked that."

She took a job as librarian for the Daily News, the smaller of two daily papers in Anchorage; the larger being the Anchorage Times, owned by the Atwood family.

Fanning turned into a reporter when she learned that the grandfather of her daughter's school friend was involved with sales of an illegal drug for treatment of cancer. Her story about that doctor made page one of the Daily News. Having started at the top, she learned the nuts and bolts of reporting by reading newspapers and studying their style. Subsequent stories—the deaths of three university students on a nearby glacier and a series on Native Alaskans—earned her top professional awards.

The following summer, she returned to Chicago and married Larry Fanning, former managing editor of the San Francisco Chronicle as well as the two Chicago newspapers owned by Marshall Field, Jr. Larry Fanning's plan was to go with her to Anchorage, stay long enough to sell her house, then head back to Chicago. But he liked what he saw and they stayed.

In the autumn of 1967, they bought the Anchorage Daily News. Larry assumed the titles of editor and publisher. His wife filled in the gaps—selling ads, reporting, and editing the paper's low-budget Sunday magazine.

Though they worked hard, the paper teetered financially. Not only was the Times well-established with twice the circulation, the Daily News backed causes unpopular with a conservative population—gun control and Native Alaskan issues—and voiced environmental concerns on the proposed 800-mile oil pipeline.

In 1971, four years after they bought the paper, Larry Fanning died there, of a massive heart attack. His wife took his place. "It never occurred to me to do anything but nurture our baby which was the paper," she said. "We went through heavy times. Often I didn't know where the payroll was coming from."

Signing a Joint Operating Agreement with the Anchorage Times in 1974 gave her breathing room. The competing paper printed, sold advertising for, and distributed the Daily News out of its new downtown plant and in return the Daily News turned over its Sunday edition.

But neither the JOA, Fanning's subsequent successful lawsuit against its terms nor a 1976 Pulitzer Prize brought financial salvation for the Daily News. That came with a deal Fanning worked out in 1979 with McClatchy Newspapers, owners of the Sacramento Bee. McClatchy would own 80 percent of the paper; Fanning would retain 20 percent—since sold—and continue to run the paper.

The Daily News flourished under the new arrangement. But in 1983, Fanning took on a new challenge. The board of directors of the Christian Science Church, owner of the Christian Science Monitor, asked Fanning to become editor.

"I couldn't believe it," she said. "I felt totally unqualified. I'd only edited a regional newspaper in Alaska. I had never handled foreign policy issues, only wire copy.

"But they insisted I was qualified and urged me to come to Boston. I guess because we'd been successful in Anchorage."

She accepted the job, coming in at the top of a veteran newsroom staff, many with 20 years and more on the paper and reporting experience from all over the world.

"I think they wondered what hit them," Fanning said. "First of all, I was the first woman editor in the history of the paper. Secondly, I was a strange soul dropped on them from the Arctic. I decided the best way to learn my job was to visit some of the areas where we had foreign correspondents. At the time, The Monitor had bureaus in seven parts of the world. It's a very particular responsibility to deal with overseas bureaus, so I visited many of them to familiarize myself with the operation and the issues. I spent two weeks in Russia, a couple of weeks in China and Japan. At that time, we didn't have bureaus in either China or Japan and I was told that one of the reasons management was sending me abroad was to decide which should have a bureau. I came back and said, 'I'm sorry, folks, but we have to have one each place.'"

Fanning ran the editorial side—news and opinion pages—of the newspaper for the next five and a half years. Overseeing content may have been the easiest of her duties. Hiring, policy-setting, dealing with the board of directors and the public, and representing The Monitor, came with her title.

Working through a change of ownership at the Anchorage paper proved valuable in her new role. Though she'd retained editorial control after McClatchy came in, for the first time, she'd answered to someone higher and initially, that was difficult. The management consultant McClatchy brought in suggested Fanning not try to run everything, not get involved in all phases of newspaper production.

During her remaining three-and-a-half years at the Daily News, she'd learned new ways of relating, backed off from quick criticisms and demands, and remembered to praise. She listened more, delegated, and solicited ideas from all employee levels.

"Since 1908, The Monitor had a tradition of authoritarian structure with an editor speaking from on high and everyone running around, doing what the editor said," Fanning recalled. "When I got there, I was astounded—horrified—by how much power I had. I don't believe in that kind of structure, so the first thing I did was set out and try to build a team; pick five or six key editors in charge of various departments and we'd manage the news side of the paper together. We had weekly meetings where we talked of problems of management, of personnel, our relations with our superiors and the business side—all these things. I needed their help. They had the institutional memory I didn't.

"The Monitor is a very small paper with a small staff, but because it is a national paper, it competes with The New York Times, Los Angeles Times, and Wall Street Journal. So part of my responsibility was to help persuade management that in order to compete in those circles, we had to pay good salaries and hire top notch people."

The paper is owned by the Christian Science Church and most of the editors and writers on it, like Fanning, are church members.

"Early on," she said, "it was determined they wanted me to hire Christian Scientists. Since I couldn't find enough really good Christian Science journalists, I had to create them. I found superb people in other lines of work—college professors, writers of another sort, or in the State Department. They became absolutely first-rate correspondents, overseas and in the U.S.

"To try to compress what I had to do there, it was, most of all, to identify top people and get them to the right place, doing the right things, and treating the right subject matter. So it required a certain amount of judgment, knowledge of people, and diplomacy—more than sitting down with a pencil and a piece of copy."

She encouraged input from her staff, becoming acquainted with them through a series of small, once-a-week lunches. Eventually, everyone had the opportunity to meet the new editor, personally and informally.

Fanning's understanding of why she'd been hired as editor of The Monitor was to build its editorial excellence. On such matters, Fanning answered directly to the five-member church board of directors which held the purse strings. In addition, she reported to The Monitor's equivalent of publisher on financial matters. He also reported to the board. That hierarchy, she said, didn't always work well.

When Fanning joined The Christian Science Monitor she headed a newsside staff of 140. By the time she left, that number had grown to 175. She'd doubled the number of foreign bureaus to 114 and increased the competitiveness of the paper's Washington bureau. But since The Monitor had been losing money, part of the challenge she faced was turning that around.

"Gradually," she explained, "or not so gradually, about a year after I came, there was a tremendous move into broadcast—first radio, then television, then a magazine. All of this drained resources from the paper.

"Furthermore, there was an expectation on the part of some people who didn't really know a lot about how writers work, to want reporters to do all three—maybe all four—media and that caused tension.

"Radio could work quite well with print. Our correspondents could tape an interview for radio after they finished a story for the paper. But television is another thing. You had to get visuals and this was a backbreaker for the staff.

"Meanwhile, the church wanted to spread the influence of The Monitor. Radio became daily. The television went from once a month to weekly to daily—which ended up costing over $20-million dollars a year to produce—to becoming a full-fledged, 24-hour, seven-days-a-week, national and international cable channel, The Monitor Channel.

"Some of us warned and warned and warned about this—this was way beyond the resources of the church in financial as well as personnel terms. At this point they were planning to cut the paper (number of pages) in half.

"I came home one night and told my husband they were going into this television venture and had turned out the lights in the underground garage to save money. I said any outfit that has to turn out the lights to get money to go into television doesn't belong there.

"They'd said they were going to cut the paper drastically and did, but I wasn't there to oversee its demise. I and my two closest associates stood up together in the newsroom and resigned and went public with why we resigned."

Her Monitor years came to an end in 1988. She remembered, with pride, a couple of series she planned. In the first, a team of two reporters traveled to 11 countries on all continents to report on women in the developing nations. That was followed by "Children of Darkness," a series about the world-wide exploitation of children as soldiers, prostitutes, and factory workers.

"We did a number of things like that which I like to think I had a part in," Fanning said. "They were my ideas and something a male editor might not have thought of."

Though Fanning entered newsroom management by marriage rather than starting at the bottom and working her way up, she was, nonetheless, unique. Few female journalists had Fanning's opportunity to implement ideas. Newsroom advancement for women proceeded along a predictable course: food, fashion, and feature writer to lifestyle editor. Not until the 1970s did women, in more than rare instances, take any kind of editorial responsibilities beyond that.

Her childhood vision of adult life, she said, certainly had not included newspaper management. "I'd been brought up the daughter of the biggest banker in Joliet. We lived in the big white house and I didn't want that. I wanted a simpler life. Then I turned around and married Marshall Field and got exactly the opposite. At Smith the idea of a career began to dawn on me, but I also wanted marriage and had a Southern mother who thought romance was the greatest thing in the world and that was high on my priority list.

"I guess at Smith, I thought it would be nice to have a career for a few years and then get married. It didn't work that way. I got married and then had a career.

"I would say that my second husband, Larry Fanning, was my role model. Actually, both my first and second husbands had a very strong sense of the role of a newspaper, of its having a dynamic and formative, important effect on the community, but probably Larry was the major influence. He was a newspaper man's newspaper man—almost a professor in the way he ran newsrooms. He discovered a lot of writers and helped them develop—Ann Landers, Mike Royko, and Georgie Anne Geyer, for example. He worked individually with his writers and they adored him."

Though a perpetual shortage of operating funds was the major problem she faced during her Alaska years, not being taken seriously because she was female was a constant irritant:

"The paper was in trouble not because I was a woman though many people thought so. The paper was in trouble because two papers were not surviving in a town of that size and the other paper was the dominant one.

"Another problem was the liberal position we'd taken. We were called things like Pravda North because we were in favor of the environment and rights of the Alaska natives and there was a very strong, rugged individualism in Alaska which Mr. Atwood personified.

"So a woman running a newspaper that had liberal tendencies and cared about people and believed there were goals in life other than making money was looked upon suspiciously."

A financial expert who came to analyze operations at the Anchorage Daily News told her, seriously and kindly, that he didn't understand why she continued to struggle with a newspaper in trouble, why she was not in her kitchen baking cookies.

"So there was always some of that," she said. "When I first became editor and publisher, twice having been married to the editor and publisher, if someone came in, particularly a man, I would move from behind my desk and sidle around to be on the same side as they were. I just wasn't comfortable in what appeared to be a power position, but I learned to be as time went on.

"I remember a confrontation with the general manager who had been general manager when Larry was alive and worked for me after he died. He presented me with a plan on how we should operate the paper, all written out very beautifully. I read it and called him in.

"'Dave,' I said, 'I really appreciate this. You've taken a lot of time and trouble. As a matter of fact, if I followed this, I wouldn't have to come into the office at all, would I?' He said, 'Well...well...'

"I said, 'I truly appreciate this, but I think I'm going to operate this paper myself.' Not long after that, he tried another ploy.

Katherine Woodruff Fanning

He'd looked for work elsewhere. I said. 'Fine. I'm sorry about that. I'll miss you very much.' From that time on, we worked harmoniously together. I was number one. He was number two.

"I had that thing with several others. I needed dynamic people and they were mostly males because they were the ones with experience. So I often ran into dynamic men, working for me, who thought they could nudge me out of the way and run the show, and we'd have to have a little showdown about that.

She saw the women's movement of the 1960s and 1970s from a distance. While she viewed it with sympathy, she didn't get involved.

"At that point, I just had a different agenda. I guess my struggle against Mr. Atwood, the publisher of the other paper, was my woman's movement because he was not only the dominant force in town, but the state. I remember when we went into the JOA, he patted me on the head and said, 'Some knight in shining armor is going to come and carry you away.' And that was his attitude.

That was what he expected of me. He didn't take me seriously and I guess he got quite a shock."

Like many other women, Fanning had not only her work but the added responsibility of raising children by herself. She said she managed her time so as to be available to them.

"Before Larry and I were married and before we bought the paper, when I was a reporter, I'd get up at 3 in the morning and write until 7, then get them off to school. I'd be home from the paper when they got home at about 3. I really tried not to let the career get in the way of what I saw as children with a great deal of need.

"They'd lost two fathers by then: Marshall Field died two weeks after we got to Alaska. There had been the divorce, my remarriage, and then Larry's death. I felt I needed to be on hand for them as much as I could be and not let my career—which I loved and which was keeping this paper going—in any way interfere with being on hand for them.

"Looking back, I guess what I consider mistakes probably would have more to do with the kids than anything else. I hauled them off to Alaska very abruptly. I didn't realize adjusting to major losses overnight was very hard for them and it was. As far as mistakes in terms of my career, I always felt rather badly about having to sue Mr. Atwood. In many ways, I liked him and kind of understood him, but it was the only way to get his attention. The way the JOA had been constructed depended entirely on his good will in making both newspapers work."

Fanning's life hadn't slowed much since those Alaska days. "Before I came to Boston," she said, "I was involved with a number of national organizations. I was on the Pulitzer Prize board and the board of the American Society of Newspaper Editors. After I came to The Monitor, I got on the ladder of the ASNE which meant that I became treasurer, the next year secretary and so forth. I was president in 1987-88 and the only woman president in its sixty-some year history, though another woman is, I hope, now on the ladder. I teach a course in journalism ethics at Boston University,

"I'm on a number of boards and a trustee of the Charles Stewart Mott Foundation which is a billion-dollar plus organization. Mott was an early General Motors founder and the foundation does work in South Africa and Eastern Europe and some in Latin America and a lot with the environment.

"I'm a trustee of the Kettering Foundation, also General Motors money. It operates a number of international programs in the U.S. and abroad. I'm also involved in the Center for Foreign Journalists, headquartered in Reston, Virginia, which trains journalists from all over the world—sends people out to do that and brings journalists in. I was founding director of the Institute for Global Ethics, out of Camden, Maine, a director of the Maynard Institute for Journalism Education; and also involved with the Freedom Forum Media Study Center.

"I married again. Just as I was leaving Alaska, I started seeing Amos, or Mo, Mathews. He was an engineer, West Point, career Army. He came to Alaska as head of the Corps of Engineers, retired there, and went into the gas pipeline business. He'd been divorced for awhile. Then suddenly, I was asked to come here to The Monitor.

"I remember when I got the job offer, I told him, 'They want me to be editor.'

"He said, 'I thought so.'

"'You did?' I said. 'It never occurred to me.'

"He said, 'Well, you're going to take it, aren't you?'

"I said, 'What about you?'

"He said, 'I might come to Boston, too.'

"And we were married in 1984, a few months after I got here. I'd told him he'd better come for awhile and see the church I was going to be involved with, this life I'd have, and see if he could handle it all right."

In spite of her subsequent falling out with its leadership, she remained very much involved with the Christian Science Church.

In the future, Fanning hopes to cut down on her activities enough to do some writing. She saved a great deal of material from her Alaskan years. There's a story in the tale of the two newspapers and the development of Alaska during the pipeline years that no one yet has told, she said. She'd like to write it in Alaska. Though she sold the house she owned in Anchorage, she and Mathews spend July and August in the condominium they bought there.

"Aging? I don't think about it."

"You asked what I regretted," she continued. "I think the few things in my life I've regretted, I've done abruptly. I ended that marriage very abruptly, but I was floundering and, at the time, leaving seemed the only way I could do it."

If Fanning ever looks back and attempts to evaluate what impact her career in newspapers has had, she might want to remember comments she made that afternoon:

"When we came, Anchorage had a population of under 100,000 which grew to about 250,000 during the pipeline years. That was half the number in the entire state and nearly all of its income.

"So how the state went was heavily influenced by what people in Anchorage thought. Juneau, the capital, was a thousand miles away, very tiny, and could only be reached by sea or a harrowing flight. A lot of information Juneau needed came from the newspaper.

"If our paper had not been there, I think the state would have gone in a very different direction. The ruling elite there was conservative, oil-industry oriented. Not that we didn't come to support pipeline development, but with balance and environmental concern.

"I really believed, and still do, that a newspaper can have a tremendous influence for good in a community—or for ill."

1 From a first-person account by Fanning in the book, *New Guardians of the Press: Selected Profiles of America's Women Newspaper Editors,* edited by Judith Clabes; published 1983 by R.J. Berg & Co.

6

Florence Crim Robinson, composer, conductor, educator; born 1932; Ph.D. Southern Illinois University; TV, radio personality; chairman arts and humanities, Callaway Professor
Atlanta University, Atlanta, Georgia.

Astatement seemed to follow her. I stumbled onto it several times, long before we met, in writings about her. "Since
I have had to overcome two handicaps, being black and
female, I have always known that merely being good in all en-
deavors was not good enough. I have worked to be the best that I
could be. It is important that I do what I feel is right for me. When
one likes and respects oneself, there is rarely much difficulty getting respect from others."

That's an upfront statement few of us put out about ourselves.
Why not? Maybe we'd have to live with that as the standard by
which we're judged? Perhaps because personal definitions make
us uncomfortable? Or maybe we haven't really figured out what
we want for ourselves, bottom-line, and what it takes to get there.

Florence Crim Robinson did, though in person she spoke
quietly and was the model of modesty. It took an after-view of her
words to see the strength and sureness of her life.

Clark-Atlanta University, where Robinson was a dean, was
in downtown Atlanta. Morning traffic had been tangled, stop and

go, and heavy. Major construction on campus had shut down some of the access streets, adding to the urban confusion.

Robinson had donated her reserved slot for us at a parking lot behind loops of orange plastic fencing and that's where she stood, waving away the car whose driver thought he'd lucked out in the morning's parking lottery.

The racket of heavy equipment, she said, was due to a new living and learning center, being built with a $20-million gift from comedian/writer/actor/director Bill Cosby. She also talked a bit about the university complex. Clark College, she said, was a part of Atlanta University Center, the largest, predominantly black consortium of schools in the world: The oldest, Atlanta University, convened classes in a boxcar shortly after the end of the Civil War; Spelman, a women's college; Morehouse, all men; Morehouse School of Medicine; Morris Brown, a four-year college; and the Interdenominational Theological Center. W.E.B. Du Bois taught at Atlanta. Fletcher Henderson, pioneer of modern jazz, and lawyer, poet, and composer James Weldon Johnson were students. The colleges, she said, owned one of the finest and largest collections of black art in the world. Current student population of all the institutions she estimated at 14,000.

Robinson was a handsome woman with thick, softly curling, shoulder-length, black hair, dark expressive eyes and honey-colored skin. That morning, she wore a black three-piece knit suit threaded with gold that matched her jewelry.

Her offices, in the Sage-Bacote building, were just along the walk from the parking lot. Sage and Bacote, Robinson said, were two great scholars. Robinson's office was one of several adjoining a central room where students and faculty stopped briefly to talk with one of the receptionists or with administrators in the other offices. The department of arts and humanities had moved in only recently, Robinson said. Her office came with undecorated, newly painted walls and no distinguishing marks, one potted plant, two visitors' chairs, desk, computer, bookcase, cabinet, two windows.

This is what she said about her work: "I wear two hats. The one I most enjoy is being the Fuller E. Callaway professor of music and distinguished chair. Fuller Callaway, Sr. made his millions in the textile industry in Georgia. The family trust endows distinguished chairs at all the colleges and universities in Georgia, and I feel honored to be that person here. Whatever your salary is, the foundation enhances it by a third more. There are about seven other distinguished professors, but they are all men. I'm the only female distinguished professor at this university.

"The appointment lasts as long as I'm around. This was done deliberately so whoever the Callaway professor was, would not be at the whim of changing administrations or afraid to speak out. Since it is a lifetime chair, this permits me a lot of freedom in terms of being creatively encouraging.

"The other hat is, I am also in charge of all the arts and humanities at the university. We have a dean of the school of arts and sciences and I am the associate dean for the arts and humanities. I've been in the dean's office since Clark College and Atlanta University consolidated in 1988. It's now Clark-Atlanta, and we have about 5,500 undergraduate and graduate students including a great number of foreign students in graduate schools, particularly from Africa and Asia.

"We have the usual studies, sociology, English, history. Many of the students are in education which I have nothing to do with. Some things are unique. For instance, Clark-Atlanta is the only school in Georgia which grants advanced degrees in library science and that attracts students from all over the state. This school is highly respected for its long history of outstanding faculty and students. I remember as a child, my father—who was in education but wound up his career as an administrator in the Illinois welfare system—used to say, 'I'd just love to go to Atlanta one summer and take some courses in their school of social work.'

"In our own school of arts and sciences we grant a graduate degree in African Women's Studies. Some of the women in it went to Nelson Mandela's inauguration; some are involved in a project to help women with AIDS in Kenya."

Robinson received her Callaway appointment in 1982 at Clark College. The previous recipient had retired and the chair remained vacant for a year.

"There was so much politicking," she said, "and I honestly was very sure they would never name anyone in the arts and humanities, because usually it's someone in the sciences. The previous person, who had been in the social sciences, was the first who was not in the sciences. I learned (about the appointment) when I was in the president's office for something else. As I was leaving, he said, 'Florence, wait a minute...' The public announcement came about three months later.

"I was in very good company. The Callaway professors here and at Emory University and the University of Georgia are truly outstanding scholars. We get together—at Callaway Gardens (Atlanta) at the invitation of the Callaway family—about once a year."

A rich professional background is a major requirement for a Callaway appointment. A pianist, Robinson has played in major halls, including Carnegie, Town Hall, Fullerton and Ganz halls in Chicago as well as performances in Denver and Atlanta. She studied the music of ethnic minorities in the People's Republic of China.

Her work on radio and television included a radio series, "The Many Sides of Black Music," and a PBS special, "The Music of Black Composers." She'd been a guest lecturer at the universities of Connecticut, Nebraska, Michigan, Massachusetts, and Southern Methodist, among others. She'd accompanied recitals throughout the world and is organist for her church.

Being a dean, she said, requires people skills. "College professors can be very difficult. And in that job, you're dealing not only with professors but students and administrators. You have to walk a certain line, but number one is having them respect you. I believe that's the reason I'm able to get things done. Sometimes people in administrative positions do not keep up. I keep up academically and, when I came, I made it clear I would at times be away on independent study."

The same year she became a Callaway professor, she received the distinguished alumna award from Southern Illinois University, the first black female so honored.

"My parents graduated from that school, too," Robinson said. "In their day, there were still great problems with (integrated) sport—not in Illinois—but to avoid problems, they pretty much kept out of the south. My father was a member of the basketball team formed by black students. One year, the university team went all the way to the national championship. When they came back, the black team trounced them. I had to tell that story at the awards ceremony.

"My brother, Bob, also a graduate before going into the Air Force, accompanied me to that ceremony. I wish my parents could have been there, they would have been so proud. My mother was alive then, but suffering from Alzheimer's. My father had died.

"My grandmother and her sister were the first black children to attend the university's laboratory school. My great-grandmother had been turned down when she tried to enroll them, but she went to the president of the college and threatened to go to the governor. They were accepted in the 1890s. So I have great ties and a great love for that school." In 1965, she returned to SIU as professor of music and later directed the Teacher Corps program.

Both sets of grandparents and her great-grandmother lived in Carbondale, Illinois, where Florence Crim grew up. "I was truly blessed," she said. "I came from a family that, for generations, had placed a great premium on education. My family were all well-educated and people who understood the value of certain kinds of contacts. My parents made sure I took advantage of everything that went on at the university. My Aunt Viola bought tickets to the concert series at the university and took me with her. As a small child, I must have been so bored, just listening. Now I wouldn't take anything to say that at 10-years-old, I heard Rachmaninoff."

I Can't Do What?

Florence was the oldest of four children. Her sister, next in age, died in childhood, of what was likely a form of meningitis. The same illness, accompanied by days of high fevers, left her brother mentally handicapped. The fourth child became a high-ranking, well-thought-of, Air Force officer.

"He was a sensitive man who had become fascinated with ROTC at university," his sister said. "Though he died later and not in the war in Southeast Asia, I believe he was a casualty of that war.

"My great-grandmother was a fabulous influence on my life. She regaled me with stories of the family." Robinson tapped a large black and white photo on a corner of her desk. "I just received this wedding picture of an older cousin's parents—a copy of a photo that's a hundred years old. Her father was the first licensed black lawyer to argue before the Supreme Court. My great-grandmother lived in western Tennessee and had been a child there shortly after the Civil War. Her parents were determined she'd go to school and she'd tell the usual kind of story about that—walking all those miles: Her brothers, when she got tired, took turns carrying her. She had two years of college at a time when few young women did. I was like her shadow, following her everywhere.

"Both of my grandmothers were strong women. They were not overtly affectionate, but I knew they were caring and they were also excellent role models. My maternal grandmother taught school but stopped when she married my grandfather. My paternal grandmother always regretted her lack of higher education. She'd married a well-educated man and her children all went to college. In her 70s, to the consternation of all these children, she went back to school."

Robinson laughed. "When I was 14, she decided I would teach her piano. I lived on the next street. She'd call and say, 'Florence, I've run into a problem on that piece. Come over here and show me what I'm doing wrong.' And I'd hop on my bike and pedal over.

"And of course my mother was wonderful—my father too.There was not a day in my life when I did not feel loved, and that I didn't know my parents wanted the best for me."

Her parents also grew up in Carbondale and both attended Southern Illinois University. Her mother taught in the city's public schools for 25 years; her father, who had been a school administrator, switched to social work. Her father, though not a musician, had a good voice and enjoyed singing. Her mother played the piano.

Florence was eight years old when they took her for her first piano lesson. "I was terribly afraid of the teacher and I'd sit there watching, in deadly fear, as she taught the child before me. She had a ruler in her hand. I did not want to get hit with it. My musical career almost came to an abrupt end because of that."

Since Carbondale schools were not integrated, Florence, like her mother and grandmother, attended the university laboratory school and Attucks, the black high school. For a short time, when her father worked in a state office, she went to junior high school in Springfield, Illinois.

Schools in Springfield were fully integrated in terms of students, but without black teachers or administrators. "I can remember as a child, I didn't know (race) was a problem. It must have been amusing, because when I was president of the drama club in Springfield, whenever a part came up I wanted, I'd take it." Her stage parents could be Anglo or Japanese, "this was of no consequence."

She recalled only one negative experience regarding race and that was not school-related. She and other blacks were excluded from an Abraham Lincoln birthday celebration. "The argument continued in the paper," she said, "with someone noting how threatening a 10-year-old was."

Teachers were influential in her life.

"I remember, particularly, an abstract thing that taught me there are always very good people all around you that you can count on. For that reason, I could really do a lot, knowing I had a support system. Coming out of junior high, black students told me, 'You're not going to be named outstanding student. That just isn't done. The white girl's going to get it.' I didn't know at the time, but there were teachers, all white—and I remember them very well—who were determined that would not be the case.

"At the little exercise, I sat there like everybody else, waiting for the girl's name to be called. They had to nudge me to get up. Those women taught me there are always going to be good people around.

"One of my teachers fit every stereotype of the old maid school teacher you could imagine. I think she even had pins in her hair. When I went to Springfield, I'd already been accelerated. But Springfield had a policy. They were going to put me back where I was supposed to be. This teacher, who I thought hated me and everybody, stood up for me.

"And in the university school in Carbondale, I also had many fine black teachers out of the better northern system. They were determined to teach their students that you could achieve, you could accomplish. Not now, but the time will come and you must be ready."

She finished high school at 14. "When I'd started, they'd decided there was no point in my sitting in classes being bored. I could read, add, and subtract, do all those things when I arrived there, because of, again, my great-grandmother. She took the Chicago Herald-American every day and when I was very small, I remember her reading me the comic pages. I think I must have been about three when she said, 'I don't have to read this to you. You can read it yourself.' That's when I learned to read.

"She would show me off. We'd go into a book store—this sounds insufferably arrogant—and the clerk would see this little girl.

"'Here's a book for you, honey,' she'd say, and hand me a 'See Jane run.' My great-grandmother had been waiting for that.

"'No,' she'd say, and reach for another one. 'Florence, read a little of this...' She loved to do that. She taught me to add too. Then she decided, and this is very good methodology, that any bright child who could add, could understand the concept of subtraction. So I learned that, too, and how to tell time. And in high school, to graduate in three years instead of four, was just a matter of going to school summers.

"I had a wonderful teacher at the university school who taught me American literature which I loved, loved, loved. They had a policy of no pluses in high school classes. She'd given me A-pluses. I learned later, she'd been called on the carpet for that. But she'd been there forever and she was like the 2,000-pound gorilla—she could do anything she wanted. She merely told them, 'If I can't give Florence an A-plus, I can't give anyone else an A.'"

Robinson set off to college with the goal of becoming the first female judge of the Supreme Court. But along with pre-law, she tried to crowd in as many arts and music courses and events as she could. At the end of the first year, an advisor said, "You've got to decide what you're going to do. You'll not be able to keep up this pace."

She decided to concentrate on music. "I knew I'd never make money in music, but that's where the love was. I became a piano major, with a minor in voice, sang in musicals, was in all the choral organizations. I played in the university symphony and had been a soloist. At first, I thought I'd be a performer—I guess all musicians think they will be. Then I realized, there were people out there better than I, though I played well as students go. I also was not sure I had the dedication to be a performer—that's an all-day, everyday, job.

"Later, when I was out of school and in Denver, studying with the legendary Dr. Antonia Brico, she'd sometimes stop me in the middle of a lesson and say, 'Why didn't you go into performing? Why weren't you that dedicated, that committed?' I told her I'd made the decision I wasn't going to do that and by then had gone too far down another path.

"I'd started teaching for one thing, and I married fairly young. He was not a musician, he was a businessman. I had the two kids and I had my hands full. There was a period there when I tried to do too much, but I always believed I could do everything."

Robinson composed in her head long before she began putting her music on paper. She started writing music in college, after being disappointed in the limitations of what she found in the music stores.

"That first year I taught, I decided to write a music version of—nothing small time about this—Dickens' 'Christmas Carol.' And I did. It probably was not so hot, but I thought it better than other things I'd heard. People began to ask, 'Would you mind my using this?' And after that I began writing all the time. I've never undertaken a big orchestral arrangement though, just solos and choral works and some piano works."

Robinson was 18 when she graduated from Southern Illinois. She started her master's at Northwestern, then left for a six-week workshop in Denver put on by Etude, a music magazine.

"When I went to Denver, it was the first time I'd had any freedom. My parents were very strict. Even at Northwestern, I'd think at any moment my father might walk in. I loved being in Denver. I'd never been in the mountains before. And that was where I met the man that I married."

The following year she transferred from Northwestern to the University of Denver where she earned her master's in music. She began work on a doctorate at the University of Colorado and taught elementary and secondary school music in the Denver Public Schools. She also became the youngest and first African-American television music teacher in the nation, telecasting half-hour programs from Channel Six in Denver to all school children in the Rocky Mountain area.

"Every Monday, Wednesday, and Friday, there I'd be: 'Hello, children...' I wrote my shows in the summer and prepared study guides that were distributed to the teachers. I could do so many things, that was the point. Even in out of the way, distant places, they'd tune me in and there would be someone with a Stradivarius. And the camera would come right in and show how you could tell this was a Stradivarius. I would try to do what a teacher in the classroom could not. Leonard Bernstein—he was visiting in Denver—came on my program. A charming, delightful man.

"I loved every minute of it. I was a ham. One program stands out in my mind—a British composer, guest teaching at the University of Colorado at Boulder, showed the children how he did the draft of an opera, a children's opera, 'Pandora's Box.' We sat on two stools. He sang the male roles and I played the piano and sang the female parts. And later, when the opera had been completed and performed, we brought in students from the University of Colorado to perform it."

She laughed. "I remember when the country's youngest symphony performer—a violinist—was going to be my guest. She would play an excerpt from a Haydn sonata and before she came on, I was going to talk about Haydn. It came time for the show and, oh, my, she wasn't there. I'd planned 12 minutes for her segment. Just before I went on, she called. 'I'm on Thirteenth Avenue. How do I get there?' As it happens, Denver has numbered streets and avenues and the PBS station was, I believe, on a street. I almost had a fit. What I did to fill in until she got there, was to tell those students more about Haydn than his mother knew about him."

Robinson stopped her television teaching when she became coordinator of music in the Denver schools and no longer had the time. Married by then, she was also raising their two children.

"Most of the things I did, I did around school schedules," she said. "I don't think I ever cheated them. I played for a very large church, but they went along. I think they liked having a mother who was never still and they knew many of the experiences they had, they couldn't have had without me.

"My husband was supportive. As a matter of fact, I don't think, with little children, I could have gotten the doctorate without that support. I think the biggest problem with my marriage was we were always extremely different. That is interesting for a time, then it gets to be difficult. Those differences became a bit much, although I really played the game. After awhile, it got to the point where he felt he just really didn't want to go on with what I was about at all. I, of course, resented that. I probably would have continued to go along, as many women do. But I had a terrible illness, so life-threatening I had one of those clinical death experiences."

Her illness was triggered by a large stone damming the kidneys. No one could find the source of the trouble. Finally her kidneys stopped working and that caused all other body functions to cease as well.

"When I hear of people having death experiences, I now know these exist," she said. "I was never given to flights of fancy, and I have no idea why this happened, but I know it did. I had the sense of going down through blackness toward some kind of light. I talked to departed relatives and I remember not wanting to leave them. I found out later I'd been clinically dead twice—once for six minutes, another time for nine minutes.

"After this experience, believe me, you are never the same. I was in an intensive care unit for five weeks and was completely debilitated for about four months. Sometime during that period, I decided, 'I'm not going to play any more games in this life.' I was going to have to be who I am. Accept me on my terms."

This happened in Dallas, where she'd gone after leaving Denver. She'd been offered a chair of music at a division of Bishop College and could also teach classes once a week.

But the job came with an atmosphere that did not suit her. When she recovered, she gave notice and left her job at the end of the term. She filed for divorce. She'd worried about the reaction of her family. But her children said, "You should have done this long ago. Don't put it on us—staying together for the children's sake."

She also worried about her parents' response. "I called them and in about two seconds I told them everything—'I need $2,000 and I'm getting a divorce.' No lectures.

"I went through the usual kinds of feelings. You're out there by yourself. But after awhile I knew I could do it.

"My former husband and I remained friends until his death. I've met interesting men since, but for whatever reasons, I haven't remarried. I think perhaps if I'd gotten married right away... But I waited. Now I've waited too long."

She joined the faculty in the School of Music at Southern Illinois University. In addition to teaching, she supervised student music teachers in the laboratory school. She was guest conductor and adjudicator through the Midwest and, by invitation, reviewed

Florence Crim Robinson

the university's educational program in Vietnam. In 1971, she became professor of music and department chairman at Clark College in Atlanta, Georgia.

Not until Atlanta did she add her voice to the women's movement. Before that, she'd been sympathetic but too involved with her family and her work. In Georgia, she attended legislative hearings on the Equal Rights Amendment, even though she knew passage was a lost cause.

"I'm not sure that all of the folks even knew what the ERA said. One woman testified that she wanted to stay on her pedestal. At that point, I had to say something."

She'd played the piano at civil rights rallies, had been named to the Colorado Human Relations Board. When James Baldwin spoke at a meeting in Denver, she'd added music. In college, she'd supported integration. But, she said, "I was never very aggressive. One time, a small thing, I was a sophomore and sophomores were required to attend a large convocation at the university. On this particular day, a sorority did this sketch in black face. I don't know what they were thinking of, I'm not even sure they knew how distasteful it was. There were a few of us attending and we just left, walked out. The president called me to his office. His daughter had been in the sorority. 'Florence,' he said, 'tell me exactly, what was it everyone was so indignant about? I knew if you left, it must have been serious.'

"I told him there were very few black students at the university. While we were trying very hard to disprove many of the stereotypes about us, it had not gotten to the point where we could laugh about them. Too many people still agreed with these stereotypes. I also told him about one of the teachers in Springfield I mentioned earlier. When we were due to study Vachel Lindsay's *The Congo*—Lindsay'd attended high school in Springfield—she called me in. 'Florence, I want you to take this home and read it and tell me if you have any feelings about our reading it aloud in class and discussing it.'

"When we got to Mark Twain, she did the same thing. I found neither one offensive. I mentioned this to the president. In this very large convocation at this very large university, too much anonymity existed. You didn't really know anything about that person next to you. In high school, they knew me, they knew what I was about and knew what I could do. I didn't feel threatened. Nothing they talked about would influence me in terms of the way I acted. But in this larger class situation, that was not the case."

Looking back, Robinson believed her first major career step was the move to Denver "because it laid the groundwork. I was the first black TV teacher, first black supervisor ever in that school system, named by the governor as one of the state's 100 most outstanding citizens. If I'd not made that move, none of these things might have happened. I thought there would be a time when I would be in charge of all the music in the Denver school system, and probably I would have become superintendent of schools. I left because I wanted the freedom of being at a university. That was part of it. Part of it was personal. I knew my personal life was becoming troubled. I was silly enough to think changing places would change the situation."

She talked about the musical environment. "Music is a very closed shop. I know many extremely talented, gifted musicians who have never made it. A lot depends on the politics of the situation: someone who likes your work, gives you that one opportunity.

"It's not easy to get that big break. Many fine young musicians go through the college. These days," she continued, "the competition is extremely stiff. You have to be very, very good at what you do to make it. Unfortunately, at the moment, I think we're seeing a down turn. There's a great deal of talk about cutting staff. When they cut back the numbers of teachers, the arts are always the first programs cut—always very expendable. After the Russians launched Sputnik, we went into science in a big way. I remember the arts were relegated to before and after school. I'd be sitting around at 4, 5—everyone else gone—trying to learn the guitar. I was one of the people from my church who went to Washington to lobby for PBS—that was during the Nixon administration. It's always under fire, constantly."

Robinson had been guest conductor on several occasions recently, among them all-state music festivals attended by 1,000 to 2,000 students. She'd published several musical works and had many more that only needed polishing. A number of her articles had been printed. Subjects included a 19th century composer, music as therapy, and a piece published by the World Council of Churches on her theory that music provided the greatest survival mechanisms for U.S. blacks.

"I go through the reviews in The New York Times and choose what piques my curiosity. I used to read a book all the way through even if I knew after the first six pages I didn't like it. That was silly. I don't do that now and I get a lot more read."

Robinson lives a 20-minute drive south from the city campus. Her mentally handicapped brother lives with her. "He's a lot of company," she said. "He knows more about some things than so-called normal people. He reads the newspaper every day. In some ways, he's almost a savant. If I'm writing, I'll say, 'What day does June 15 come on?' He tells me and that's what I put down because he knows. But if I were to give him a $5 bill and ask him to get this or that at the grocery store, he couldn't do it.

"But he's a wonderful person and can't do enough for me. 'Florence Claire? Do you want such and such?' He is the kindest, gentlest, most wonderful person. The only time he becomes a problem is when I have to be away, then I must have someone look in, to be certain there is enough food and there is not a crisis.

"He has his own money. My parents provided for him. They did not wish him to be institutionalized. My children are as determined as I that he won't be."

She looks forward to writing more, both music and articles. She doesn't plan to ever stop doing some teaching. "Students seem to enjoy my classes," she said. "Through the years, I've worked toward more interesting presentation and I try not to teach anything in isolation. When I teach music of the Renaissance, I include art and politics of that time as well.

"I'm not sure I'll stay in Atlanta. I don't like the pace of a large city. The other thing is, I have certainly what are the world's most delightful grandchildren. My daughter, who lives in Tallahassee, has three. I've never gotten the university town out of my system and there's a university there. I've already been told I could teach a class. I may retire in Florida.

"I sometimes do wonder if I should have stayed in Denver. I was on a path there—everyone in town knew me and I could pretty much write my own ticket. The University of colorado would call every semester. 'What classes do you want to teach?' I've sometimes had regrets. But maybe it wasn't a mistake. I'm not sure I would have ever achieved the personal freedom there I achieved by leaving. I never question the divorce. Once I almost regretted saying no instead of yes to a later marriage proposal. In hindsight, though, I don't think so. He turned into a real grump as he grew older."

Aging seemed more of a problem at 50 than it did at 60, Robinson said. "I thought then, 'Everything's behind me now.' I share a birthday with a good friend and since that year was difficult, we celebrated together, at her home in Galveston. But once it was over, I realized that while things would be different, they would not necessarily be bad or unpleasant. I put up with changes in my appearance and in my health. I adjusted. It's wonderful, I know, to be young, but there are advantages to age."

The hundreds and hundreds of young people she'd taught, the many who went on to become teachers and professionals she considered as her greatest career accomplishment.

Favorite composers? "I try never to miss a symphony by Brahms—one of my favorite orchestral composers; Mozart; I love jazz, Duke Ellington, Dizzy Gillespie. Verdi and Puccini are favorites in opera. I love the spirituals and I think they are greatly underestimated. There are some fabulous black composers who've not been recognized—the late Florence Price who did chamber music of all kinds and was the first black woman to play her work in Chicago. The Chicago Symphony and also other major orchestras performed her music. In 1910, she taught on this campus. She was Florence Smith then. The Gershwin brothers picked the late Eva Jessye—my dear friend, who died at 95—as choral director for 'Porgy and Bess,' and she was the first ever to do work for a musical film. That was the King Vidor production of 'Hallelujah.'

"Music opened a lot of doors for me. As a teenager, I was asked to perform at a reception given by Governor Adlai Stevenson. Until he died, I'd hear from him. I also played at events for Presidents Truman and Johnson.

"I think what I'm proudest of is that people whom I admire and respect, respect me. I go across the country and many know me. I don't get the kinds of reaction I see many people getting at readings and forums. It seems to me that even when others don't agree with me, they respect me.

"It's been a wonderful life," Robinson said. "It doesn't come free."

7

Denise Scott Brown, architect, planner; born
1931, Zambia; studied in South Africa, England and U.S.; eight honorary degrees; many
awards; taught architecture, planning, urban
design Un. of Pennsylvania, U.C. Berkeley,
UCLA, Rice, Yale, Harvard; principal Venturi, Scott Brown and Associates, Philadelphia.

The internationally renowned architectural firm of Venturi,
Scott Brown and Associates hid in a tall, narrow, red brick
and wood building, plain, identifiable only by a number on
a recessed door and a sign on another pointing to a side entrance.
Neighbors on the narrow street in Manayunk, a Philadelphia ap-
pendage, included a dog groomer, dessert shop and counter-cul-
ture boutiques.

Past the door at the top of three unremarkable flights of stairs,
a long counter opened into a room of people and tables under a
ceiling of fluorescent tubes.

Denise Scott Brown was in a meeting. We waited in a corner
at the opposite end from the workroom. Fraser sat in a red, straight-
backed, armless chair that looked cut out of plywood. On the wall
behind him, a framed poster commemorated Venturi, Scott Brown
and Associates, Architecture and Decorative Art, Kyoto, June 30,
1991. The chair on the poster was the same as the one below it.

96

On a shelf opposite, a thick, glossy book, *The Japan Architect*, sat next to a model of a house with walls of coconut cookies and vanilla wafers; windows of cookies with jam centers; a roof of animal crackers.

A nearby door opened and a half dozen people filed out. I recognized Denise Scott Brown from photos. Her hair, once red, was white and cut shorter. In life, she seemed smaller. She looked at us over the top of half glasses above high cheekbones. We followed her into the room she'd left and sat around a long table. Architectural drawings and colored renderings leaned against the walls and were pinned up at eye level. A building, modeled of paper, sat on a shelf at one end. Around the room were a dozen or more poster chairs, all colors, some with crazy patterns or bright fabric cushions.

Scott Brown spoke entrancingly—her accent an honestly acquired mix of English-speaking South African and Oxford-Cambridge. Born in Nkana, Zambia, she grew up in Johannesburg, studied architecture at the University of the Witwatersrand, South Africa, and the Architectural Association in London. She earned master's degrees in city planning and architecture at the University of Pennsylvania.

"My husband (Robert Venturi) and I are the owners of our firm," she said, "and as such, I work in both architecture and planning and also in the management of the firm. At the moment, we have about 50 employees."

In addition to her work in architecture and planning and management, she considers herself the firm's chief strategist. "We don't have a manager partner, we all share it, and I probably work out how we all share it.

"I probably contribute most by bringing urban thinking and an urban scale to architecture. Taking the civic indoor is another way of describing it. A city plan is a plan for a pattern of activities before it is a prescription for buildings and streets. You can think of a building that way, too. When you focus creatively on the pattern of activities in a building you become an analyst and designer of situations before you are a designer of rooms and corridors."

The way all of this evolved for her, she said, came from a great variety of people who'd been important in her life—"my father, 30 maybe 40 teachers. When I studied in England, a movement called New Brutalism had started in the 1950s and as students of the Architectural Assocation in London, we felt a part of it."

Basically, New Brutalists searched for social involvement through architecture and accompanied that with critiques of contemporary architecture as well as that of the 1930s and 1940s.

"An old German refugee from the Bauhaus, Arthur Korn, who taught at the Architectural Association, was extremely supportive, a very important influence," Scott Brown said. "His view tied social questions to architectural ones and that was important to me before I met him and has been ever since.

"Also important in my intellectual development was an ethnomusicologist, Charles Seeger. I met him in my 30s. He was in his 70s, an emeritus professor at the University of California at Los Angeles. He was doing in his field what I was trying to do in mine—tie artistic questions to social ones. He was 40 years ahead of me so there was much I could learn from him.

"And then my mother. She'd studied architecture and I grew up thinking it was woman's work. I wanted to be an architect before I ever went to grade school, but there I found a mother surrogate and wanted to be a teacher. Later, I wanted to study languages and write.

"A few years ago I looked back at all those things I wanted to do and realized I'd done them all. But always within the framework of architecture. That's my window on the world."

When she left South Africa in 1952, she left behind Robert Scott Brown. Both were architectural students and South African training required an interning year. She chose to do that in England, newly accessible after World War II.

"I had thought I'd work my fourth year in London and then go back to South Africa," she said, "but partway through I realized I had this opportunity to study at the Architectural Association. I took the exam, and when I got in, I felt fate pushing me. I decided to stay and graduate at the AA before going back to South Africa. Robert joined me when he finished and we got married. We did a small course in tropical architecture in London. After that we'd go back. But then we believed we should have more training. Who knew if we'd ever get out again? And the training we believed we should have more of was city planning. One of the New Brutalists advised us to study under Louis Kahn who was teaching at the University of Pennsylvania."

As it turned out, Kahn taught in the university's architecture department, not in city planning where they enrolled in 1958.

Of that time, she wrote, "Robert and I...went twirling around in a whirl of intellectual excitement. We didn't know how we could have lived our life till then without all that information." [1]

Though architecture had been her major focus, a growing interest in city planning gave her career a slightly different spin. Then, following Robert Scott Brown's death in an automobile accident in 1959, her life and career turned again.

"My husband's death shattered the plans we'd made together," she said. "In the confusion that followed, the only clear indication was that I had every good reason to go on with my studies. When they were over, it just seemed the next step was to start teaching and I went from there."

From 1960 to 1965, she was an assistant professor in Penn's School of Fine Arts. She left because she was not reappointed, and left angrily after finding she had earned less than colleagues with the same academic background, less even than newly graduated students she'd taught.

The University of California at Berkeley invited her to be one of its visiting professors and she stopped there for a semester. Then, in 1965, she went on to help set up the School of Architecture at the University of California at Los Angeles. Though she'd been offered tenure, she said, once there it didn't happen.

Scott Brown moved to a house on the beach and informed university heads they'd find her there—writing the book they told her she needed for tenure. She wouldn't be back until she got that and wouldn't accept assistant professor pay level either. Eventually a settlement was negotiated—though tenure was not a part of it.

Among the speakers she invited to her classes was Robert Venturi. As a faculty member at the University of Pennsylvania, she'd been impressed by his course on the theories of architecture. He'd since moved to Yale.

In Los Angeles, they took a weekend to look at the architecture of Las Vegas. They returned fascinated with what they'd seen and in love. In an account of those years, [2] Scott Brown recalled she didn't announce their engagement until she got tenure. She then resigned and in 1967, she and Venturi married. She returned to Philadelphia and joined the architectural firm of Robert Venturi and John Rauch.

Scott Brown said she'd been a feminist since the 1940s and 1950s, but it was her experience as an architect married to an architect that turned her into an activist.

"I remember arguing with German students when I was traveling in Spain in 1953. One said he'd never allow his wife to work. I thought it outrageous that he'd said that. How could you dictate to someone? Even before that, I was always careful to put my full name on my drawings in architectural school so they'd know it had been done by a woman.

"And in the mid-60s, when I had trouble getting tenure, that was because I was a woman. But I loved the ratio in every school where I was: one woman for every 12 men. That meant I got a great deal of attention which I liked.

"I used to say, 'I'm a woman who prefers the company of men.' Then I found there were women who, like me, preferred the company of men, and I said, 'Well, I like those women.' At the time, I was pretty scornful of talk about kitchens and children.

Suddenly, those who preferred the company of men and of other women like themselves joined women's lib."

But being the unrecognized contributor to Venturi and Rauch projects focused her sense of being treated unfairly based on her sex. As a member of the firm, she'd go to interviews and find the presence of "the architect's wife" bothered the board. At business dinners, she'd be excluded because one of the client group wanted the architect as her date. A continuing source of irritation were projects done jointly but, in published articles, attributed only to Venturi.[3]

When critics wrote about "his" work when it was "their" work she fired off angry letters to the press, saying did they think she was her husband's typist?

"And then," Scott Brown continued, "I remembered my father telling about the German Jews who felt they were different from the Eastern Jews and the Spanish Jews who said, 'we're not like other Jews, we're Spanish.' These Jews found themselves eradicated as much as anyone else.

"I realized it really doesn't make sense to say 'I'm different from other women' and I began to say, 'If any of us is to be emancipated, all of us must be.' There's no way I can say I'm different from the secretaries. And when I became a mother, I found I had a whole lot to talk about with other people who were raising children.

"At this point, I believe women who choose to be at home, to raise children, to work as housewives, are executives; probably as much or more than their husband working in a firm. That's a choice they have a right to make."

Professionally, she and Venturi had been controversial because they condemned and ignored accepted design doctrine. Their book, *Learning from Las Vegas,* (MIT Press, 1972) caused a good deal of comment, as might be imagined from the title. Basically they argued that the "theme-image-role-playing signs" along the Las Vegas strip were a legitimate architectural attraction. Architecture is as much symbol as form, they wrote.

Criticisms of *Learning from Las Vegas* that she resented most were those that declared, "'How can you tell architects to be nonjudgmental? If people had been nonjudgmental in the past, we'd still have slavery and segregation.'

"That, I think, is stupid. We don't say you should be nonjudgmental about everything. We're talking specifically about architecture and a phase in the process—delaying judgment to make judgments more sensitive.

"I still get holier-than-thou people who say, accusingly, 'You like gambling.' My answer to that is, 'I certainly don't like medieval Christianity, but I love Chartres Cathedral.' No. I don't like gambling and I don't do it.

"Others say, 'You're being used by the capitalist imperialists.' Others that Las Vegas is visual pollution. That's wrong headed. We say chemical pollution is something that can be measured in the air and in the water, but one person's visual pollution is another's visual delight."

"Startling" was a word that frequently showed up in regard to work by Scott Brown and Venturi. Or did their theories provoke that description?

"Both, I think." she replied. "First it is startling that you could learn from Las Vegas and then startling that you might not be a Modern architect in the traditional sense. We say we're not Postmodernists, we're Modernists. We use decoration and symbols that are startling to people who had expected Modern symbolism to be veiled. Modernism does have symbolism, but the architects let it in by the backdoor. The International style was intended to shock. Its stark white buildings said, 'Modern life should be like this, not like the over-decorated buildings of the late 1890s.' Architects stripped off all the decorations, but this was just another form of symbolism."

At that time, her list of favorite creations included the National Gallery in London and the Seattle Art Museum, though her personal involvement had been greater in the former. Scott Brown's credits included the architectural program for the National Museum of the American Indian and plans for downtown Memphis; Washington Avenue in Miami Beach; Jim Thorpe, Pennsylvania; the Denver Civic Center Cultural Complex; Houston Museum of Fine Arts; parts of Dartmouth College campus; and the University of Pennsylvania campus.

Though the South Street project of 1968 never became reality, it encompassed many of Scott Brown's professional beliefs. Venturi and Rauch were hired by a Philadelphia citizens' committee who wanted to prevent the construction of an expressway through their neighborhood. This would have replaced the existing main street, South Street, through the inner-city black community. Scott Brown's plan proposed that the community control local planning, guiding land use development for their benefit. South Street would be commercially rehabilitated. Existing buildings would be renovated, where possible, for low-income ownership; rental housing, streets, sidewalks and parking would be improved.

The South Street concept of inner-city development hadn't inspired others. "Unfortunately," she said, "the idea of democratic participation in planning was taken up by other groups, often upper middle-class communities, who want to keep the poor out, who believe their taste is the only good taste and don't want the vulgarity of someone else's. Community involvement seems to have been taken over by a small segment of the society and is being used for their particular agenda. I haven't heard the poor mentioned in community meetings for 20 years."

However, the ideas of the South Street plan showed up later in Venturi and Rauch projects in California and in Philadelphia. But at least for the present, Scott Brown had left urban planning.

"I'm not teaching or practicing planning for a sad reason: The policies of a succession of presidents starting with Nixon have eroded support for the field," she said. "There's been so little investment for so many years, it's dwindled in schools and in practice. In some planning agencies when consultants are hired, there's not enough data to do the job. My last urban planning project was a plan (in the mid-1980s) for downtown Memphis. I couldn't subject our firm to losing that much money again. Planning tends to take on the coloration of the society around it. In the 1960s, planners became deeply involved in social planning. That's when I came in, finding it very sympathetic to my way of thinking.

"Then the natural world and ecology became important. After that preservation, then health sciences and the whole medical field, where planners became health planners. This is so in many areas. People go where the money is. Sociologists left planning years ago because there's no funding for it. Recently, I've been doing campus planning."

Scott Brown said what she enjoys most about her work is its mix of challenges. "Architecture, of course, is the major part of my work, but I'm thrilled to find myself working at the level of jewelry design and regional planning. A colleague used to say, 'Architects who think they can design everything from a teaspoon to a region have delusions of grandeur.' And I agree with him, but at the same time, we do all that.

"It involves a change of hats. Designing a teaspoon, you don't think the way you do as a planner."

Venturi, Scott Brown's most controversial work may have been the National Gallery in London which precipitated what architectural critics there called the second battle of Trafalgar. More recently they designed a Manhattan ferry terminal with an enormous clock which immediately moved into the mythology of New York. It inspired cartoons everywhere, Scott Brown said. "The cartoon I liked best pictured two people in a small boat going by this very, very, large clock. One said to the other, 'If the alarm goes off, it wakes five boroughs.' But the clock isn't going to happen. It's too controversial.

"To be in our 60s and still controversial is an achievement, but also frustrating and makes our lives sad and difficult. The worst is, those things we think are right but can't get built, ten years from now they'll be done, but not by us."

Projects at the time of the interview included an orchestra hall for Philadelphia; a governmental center in Toulouse, France;

Denise Scott Brown

a hotel and spa for the Ministry of Post and Telecommunications in Japan.

"Architecture is not to do with startling," Scott Brown said. "It's a matter of using every ability you have and all the help you can get to interpret what the nature of the real problem is; of being proud to take that problem and deal with it as it really is—not push it under the rug.

"Then to pull out of it something beautiful. Because urban conditions are difficult in America today, even for institutions like the orchestra, we have limitations on what we can do: a tight site, perhaps, which must be used efficiently, or a budget we wish could be higher but shouldn't be because money is needed for housing or other essentials. The kind of beauty that comes out of a design program defined in this way may be a rather agonized beauty. That's why some of the projects we design are startling. We try to approach them logically and not fudge and then the design comes out with an edge to it. The edge will make it alive, but it also horrifies for the first 20 years of its existence.

"Who in a democracy speaks for the future? Politicians usually speak for the next two years, yet as the people's elected representatives, they should also speak for the future, but they seldom do. Then what happens to the arts? Art, by its nature, speaks to the future as well as the present and some great art is hated at first. When the Eiffel Tower was built, the elite of the day—300 of them—sent a horrified letter to the government saying don't build this thing: 'For the Eiffel Tower, which American commercialism itself would not want, is, without any doubt the dishonor of Paris. Everyone knows it, everyone says it...'[4] In the first 20 years, many people may have felt that way. Ever after, people have loved the Eiffel Tower—most people, not just the elite.

"As an artist, what do you do? You're talking for the future, perhaps not even consciously. Consciously, you're trying to solve a problem today. From experience, we've discovered that what we do now will be done by other architects ten years from now and will be liked by the public 20 years from now. So we speak for the future, even if we don't intend to. But how do we get the support now to do that? Our designs of the 1960s and 1970s that may look timid now, took enormous courage to do then and we took huge hits. Yet people ask, 'What was all the fuss about?'"

Then into her seventh decade, Scott Brown hadn't slowed professionally. "We have a huge degree of pressure," she said. "When I taught, there was a sequence to the semester, particularly in architecture: You don't just give a series of lectures, you run a studio with due dates for work, jury times, exams. At semester's end, there'd be a low pressure time and I'd regenerate. I used to. And when Bob and I started working together, in this office, we still had the semester because we were teaching part time at Yale. We'd go from the office pressures—spring in the office is always very hectic—to the spring semester. It's years since we've had any down time.

"An exception would be once a year when we go to Switzerland to visit my parents. When our son, Jimmie, was small, we'd also go to Venice and take my mother with us and friends would come from Switzerland and Italy and join us and we'd have a wholly different type of life—going from street cafe to street cafe and drinking coffee and enjoying our friends. But when we travel, even for work, we're doing only one thing and that's a change."

Scott Brown returned to South Africa in 1970 with Venturi, on what she called a sentimental trip to her childhood. Her parents moved to Switzerland from South Africa in 1961. In those days of apartheid, South Africa had been an outcast among the nations of the world. "I think it was understood that we children would need to make our lives elsewhere. They could live out their lives in South Africa, but if they wanted us to find another way to live, they had to move."

Since the early 1970s, Scott Brown and Venturi have made their home in an old, 12-room house two or three miles from their office. They usually leave work about 7. Their evenings are quiet. "We watch television and go to bed early," she said. "We don't read much. To wind down, he does the Philadelphia Inquirer cross-word puzzle and I do the cryptogram."

At one time, when their son was a child, she'd written there was no time at all for outside interests. Had this changed, now that he was grown?

"There's less," she said. "At about that time, our partner retired and, to the extent that he had been managing, we then had full management responsibility. We now work weekdays and weekends. Our social life comes through our work. But that's not all bad. We go to Japan to do work and that's much more fun than being a tourist."

She had no plans to retire. "Architects get their opportunity in life late. Most die with their boots on. We have made major changes in this firm over the past decade, in the way of allocating responsibilities. We control the firm, but we have excellent project managers who know when to ask advice of us and when not to. It's an achievement to get things working that way, but for all that, we can't see a time when we won't be needed.

"Bob feels the practice of architecture has become far more difficult over the past decade. There are so many more regulations and requirements. Clients demand more. The FAX pushes you to do four times as much between meetings as you did before. Documents travel back and forth between meetings, full time. It used to be you went to interviews for jobs. Sometimes now, ten firms write book-length proposals for one job and even after that, there's a design competition. All that is expensive. It keeps us extremely occupied but not productively."

Might she cut back on the number of days she worked? "You can't do what we're doing here a few days a week," she said. "Someone asked us the other day, 'If we really told you to be visionary, what would you do?' You can't be visionary only on Friday mornings. That's what we told them. In any case, for us being visionary includes looking at hard reality. Also we knew they'd bring back the hard reality later, so why even talk about the vision thing? But if that's how you define vision, you really can't do it three days a week.

"So, I suspect if we wanted to cut down, we would have to do something else and one day, I could see myself quite happy getting some writing done. I don't get time now."

Does she look back and see mistakes? "I don't think I've made any really major mistakes, though the death of my first husband resulted in a major deflection and change. The verdict is never out on your child-rearing, even if your kid is out and about and in his 20s. Jim's a challenging person. It seems he'll be OK. He went to New York at an early age and set himself up in business. He's a computer consultant and consults mainly with architects. He supplies them with computer systems and trains them, does specialized jobs for them. And right this moment, with or without further education, he's on his way to the University of Kentucky to give a lecture on computers. We say, 'He doesn't do what we did as kids, he does what we do now.'"

Scott Brown had written accounts of her difficulties gaining recognition for her work and what she saw as its arbitrary suppression in relation to Venturi's. I wondered if an independent practice might have served her better.

"That's hard to tell," she said. "My type of intellect and creativity likes support—backing from other people who think in parallel lines. I like orchestrating the collaboration of people in different fields. I could have led that type of group and maybe gotten more attention. But at the time I was directing teams of planners, I was a woman on my own. I don't think I would have been given the opportunity outside academe in the 1960s.

"My argument against affirmative action as it's done now is that it tends to keep women and minorities in very small offices. I've integrated one of the world's great offices, but we get no affirmative action consideration because I don't own 51 percent of it. If affirmative action had a way to get minorities and women into major firms, into major positions in large firms, this would be at least a good alternative."

Brown, unlike most women interviewed, aggressively pursued what she believed to be her rights if these were, in her eyes, violated. Writers—and many sought her out—usually described her as outspoken and controversial. Listening to her bore that out. Though her hair had turned white, a quintessentially red-haired personality operated beneath it.

Her answer to a final question seemed to cover her approach to life as well as her profession: Did she believe gender made a difference in architecture?

"It certainly does in how you're treated. But are there, in fact, innate gender differences between men and women architects? We need at least 30 more years of the women's movement, and fighting it out, and acculturation, before we can answer that question.

"Feminists have battled on both sides of it. Some say there are differences and they want to promote them. Others say there aren't differences and you have to treat us the same. As a Jew, I certainly know that ambivalence. I demand that I have the same opportunities as everyone else in this society, and I demand that I be able to be myself as well. Young African-Americans today want black studies programs and the opportunities available in society at large as well. It is very logical to want both. My feeling is, it certainly should be open to blacks, Hispanics, women—any oppressed group—to be separate as well, *if* they want to be.

"When I was teaching during the Free Speech Movement at Berkeley, I failed half my class in the first test. I said, 'You're a group of bright kids, but you're not working. Here are the results and you can see you're not working.' And they hated me. But by the end of the semester, they were proud of what they'd done. I felt students had a right to be as they were then, in revolt, and I, by the same token, had a right to fight them. They had their role. I had mine. Two roles existed and I had to claim mine—it didn't matter what I'd been as a student.

"Women and minorities are justly angry today and are sometimes like my students of the 1960s. And the faculty has to have empathy, but nevertheless, when necessary, fight them—fight them lovingly and energetically, for their sakes, holding hands as they do."

1 *Particular Passions* by Lynn Gilbert and Gaylen Moore; Clarkson N. Potter, Inc.; Page 313.
2 IBID; Page 316.
3 *Architecture: A Place for Women*; edited by Ellen Perry Berkeley; Smithsonian Institution Press; Page 239.
4 *Paris: A Century of Change* by Norma Evenson; Yale University Press; Page 132.

8

Patricia McGowan Wald, Circuit Judge, U.S. Court of Appeals, District of Columbia Circuit; born 1928; law degree Yale; more honorary degrees than space; member of numerous prestigious boards; author.

The U.S. Courthouse in Washington, D.C., is pillared, enormous, and tremendously impressive. "We hold these truths to be self-evident...," words memorized in childhood, seen again on a tall column in front of the building. A camera crew set up on the broad steps. Easter was over, but a young woman shepherded a couple of pre-schoolers, baskets in hand, diving into bushes bordering the lawn between steps and sidewalk.

We went through a door for visitors and answered questions at the security check-in. A guard rang Judge Wald's chambers to find out if she'd approved cameras and tape recorder. Several floors up, the elevator doors opened onto an empty, dim, and cavernous corridor. A lone passerby sent us left, right, left, along a blank-walled hall to a panel of names and buzzers by a locked door.

A secretary led the way along another hall into a large outer office with twin desks and a pair of windows. Matisse and Jasper Johns shared wall space with a dramatic black and white photo of the courthouse, an angle shot of columns and strong shadows. *Henri*

I Can't Do What?

Matisse: The Early Years in Nice anchored a coffee table in front of the couch.

The judge's office was just beyond. Windows behind her desk overlooked Constitution Avenue. Featured elsewhere were leather-bound books, family photos, mementoes, and contemporary art. Her husband, Robert Wald, a partner in a Washington legal firm, collected the art, the judge said later. She retained veto power over what made it to her office walls.

We talked in a small, adjacent conference room, remarkable only for the sheer volume of paper it held. Judge Wald wore a black skirt, white blouse and red blazer. Her hair was black. She was short, not more than 5-feet.

Articulate and forthright, Wald answered questions—beginning with her early history—without hesitation.

"I grew up in a little town in Connecticut—Torrington—about 30 miles northwest of Hartford. It was a mill town with a lot of factories. I came from a working class, Irish-American family. My grandparents came over from Ireland. My mother was born here. My mother and my aunts all went into the local factories or offices. I was the first person in my family to have gone to college and I went on scholarships.

"My relations were, in retrospect, very intelligent people, but they were not allowed the opportunity to get formal educations. I was an only child. My father disappeared during the Depression. He was an alcoholic, I am told. I never saw him again, and I don't think my mother did either. And of course in those days, there was no support, or relief, or Aid to Dependent Children. My mother moved back with her family—my grandparents and several aunts and uncles—so I grew up in this very large, extended family, all closeted together in a very small house. My mother went back to work, and she worked all the time I was growing up so I was pretty much left on my own."

Pat McGowan learned to read early. During a succession of summers, she worked her way through the children's section of Torrington's public library. Children could only check out a book a day. She read one a day. By the time she was old enough to move on, she'd read every book in the children's department.

"I went to a parochial school the first eight years," Wald said, "and the nuns were good about pushing you, encouraging you to develop your talents, if they thought you were smart.

"I remember one thing, which in retrospect may have been important—one of those watershed decisions. When you went from parochial school into high school—we only had one high school in town and that meant about a hundred in each class—you had to sign up for a particular course.

"This was almost an educational caste system. If you were going on to college, you signed for the college course. That was for all the kids whose parents were executives or in management at the factories. Or you could sign for a normal course and the smarter of the working class kids went for that. That meant you'd become a teacher or nurse. Or you could take the business course which meant you could go into the factories and be a secretary or a file clerk, like my mother and my aunts. Boys at that level took the technical course, to become machinists.

"I'd always assumed since we had no money, literally no money, I would sign up for the normal course. But my mother and the nuns all said, 'Oh no. You're going to sign up for the college course.' Nobody knew how I was going to go to college. I didn't know. But they insisted I sign up. So I took the algebra and the Latin along with the kids who knew they were going to college. And that made all the difference. I know the number two person in my high school, a very, very, bright girl, took the business course and became an executive secretary.

"My mother made this decision without really knowing how it could be accomplished. But a rich woman in the town, whom I had never met, endowed a full scholarship for one female student out of the public high school each year. I got that scholarship. It didn't pay for everything, but I worked and my mother helped out."

Wald is now a federal judge, Circuit Court of Appeals, District of Columbia Circuit. She described that this way: "The federal judicial system is broken down into 11 circuits, each of which has jurisdiction over federal cases in a particular region. The D.C. Circuit is slightly different. It has actual geographical jurisdiction only over the District of Columbia.

"The circuit is separate because D.C. is the seat of the federal government with all the major agencies and the President and Congress here, so we have a great number of appeals from regulatory agencies—for instance, the National Labor Relations Board, Securities and Exchange Commission—as well as the main departments of the government. That's where we get our business and therefore, despite the fact we have a narrow geographical jurisdiction, we have lots and lots of cases.

"The nature of the work I do is to decide appeals; over 50 percent of those appeals come directly from agencies. Let me give an example: Supposing the Environmental Protection Agency promulgates a regulation about how many particles of a certain kind of substance from a certain industry can be emitted into the air according to the Clean Air Act.

"If the industry thinks EPA has gone beyond its authority, or that it doesn't have the evidence to support the certain kind of regulation that it promulgated, or hasn't done it in the right way by giving everyone a chance to participate in the rule-making, then the industry can bring a challenge to that regulation and appeal it to our court. On the other side of the aisle, if an environmental organization thinks EPA hasn't gone far enough, it can bring a challenge to the regulation on the same grounds. Very often we get appeals on environmental regulations in which both sides are appealing.

"We decide cases like that in the labor and management field as well and many of the regulations Health and Human Services puts out about Medicare and Medicaid payments. We also get appeals from the trial court which is in this same building. Those would often be criminal cases. We have a relatively large criminal jurisdiction; Title VII of the Civil Rights Act—gender, race and even old age; a lot of Freedom of Information cases—people asking the government for documents; and a little bit of private contract action—X suing Y. The reason for our getting that is if X and Y came from different jurisdictions.

"Though primarily we do appeals from administrative agencies, we've had a lot of high-profile criminal cases—the Oliver North case, the Marion Barry case.

"Most of the independent counsel cases come here because the independent counsel division—that's the special prosecutor—operates out of this court. That's why the Iran-Contra and HUD investigations and others end up here."

When the appeals court gets a case, Wald explained, a panel of three judges hears arguments by lawyers from each side, sometimes from an intervening group as well. What judges review is the way the decision by the lower court or agency was reached, not always the merits of the case itself. Were legal errors made? The ruling is made by the three-member panel. However, if the entire court decides a panel decision is in error, that decision can be overruled by a majority vote.

In the course of several hundred cases a year, Judge Wald estimated that only six would be heard by the full court and even fewer panel decisions reversed. Appeals Court decisions can be carried to the Supreme Court by the defendants, but few—an average of only one a year—are accepted for that ultimate level hearing. Panel decisions usually are the last word.

The judge pointed to a photograph on a shelf at the end of the room: "Over there you can see our court. At various times, we've had 11 or 12 people. We're authorized for 12, but it seems we never quite get the full 12. There's always a vacancy.

Well-known individuals have come through the District of Columbia Circuit Court of Appeals. Among them are Robert Bork, Justice Antonin Scuria, Justice Clarence Thomas, Justice Ruth Bader Ginsburg, Ken Starr, prosecutor for the Whitewater investigation.

The president appoints judges to the U.S. Courts of Appeals and his appointments are confirmed by the judges who sit in the court. Terms are lifelong.

"People who are appointed to the federal court are generally in their late 40s, 50s—occasionally in their 60s or late 30s," Wald said. "They've generally had a legal career already, been a practicing attorney or maybe a teacher of law."

When she was appointed in 1979, Wald had been a practicing attorney in the District of Columbia, primarily in public interest law. She'd already had two stints in government law—in the early 1960s in the Department of Justice as a staff lawyer under Robert Kennedy; at the time of her appointment, she was assistant attorney general for legislative affairs under President Jimmy Carter.

A career on the bench was not something she'd worked toward from an early age.

"I started out with fairly traditional notions," the judge said. "I was pretty good at math in high school and started out as a math major at college (Connecticut College for Women). Though I wasn't sure what kind of career I'd have, I thought it likely to be research involving math.

"But in my second year, I took political science from a very charismatic teacher—who made us read The New York Times before class—and got interested in government and public policy issues."

Her interest was reinforced by working summers in Torrington factories.

"This was just after the war (World War II) and, for the first time, we were again getting strikes," Wald said. "I had an uncle, in our same house, a factory worker, and he was on strike. My aunts were in the office. They were management. Although I was a temporary employee, I got very involved with the union and soon switched my college major to government.

"I'd done very well in college—I was Phi Beta Kappa—and in my last year, I was encouraged to go on to graduate school. I didn't have any money, but there were fellowships. It seemed to me a Ph.D. in government would lead to teaching, and I did not feel any vocation. A couple of my professors, who were again extremely supportive, suggested law school."

The only lawyers Wald had encountered were the father and brother of a high school friend and not much knowledge of the profession had filtered through from them.

But she passed tests for law—the first year these had been offered—then applied to several law and graduate schools. A personal essay and endorsements qualified her for a Pepsi Cola fellowship, good for wherever she wanted to go and enough to cover tuition and expenses which she would supplement with job earnings. She headed for Yale.

"I got out of law school and again had a great break," Wald continued. "In 1951 there were not lots of jobs open for woman lawyers. There had been about 10 women in my law class, which was many more than you'd ordinarily find. Until the 1970s, only a few women studied law. My best explanation was that it was a post-war class and several of the women were there on the GI Bill.

"At the time I graduated, it was almost unheard of for a woman to get a clerkship. That's working for a judge for a year, and it's a very good ticket for a future job. Jerome Frank, a well-known and wonderful man, was sitting in the second circuit which convenes in New York. A couple of the professors suggested he take me as his clerk, and he had an adventurous spirit and did."

Frank had been head of the Securities Exchange Commission during President Franklin Roosevelt's New Deal era. After Wald's year with him was over, Frank wrote letters to various law firms, suggesting Wald as a likely candidate for them. Thurman Arnold, Abe Fortas, and Paul Porter had founded a law firm a few years earlier. They hired Wald based on Frank's recommendation.

At about the same time, Wald married a law student she'd met at Yale. The year she clerked in the court of appeals, Robert L. Wald clerked in a district court. A member of the Naval Reserve, he'd missed combat in World War II but was called back for service on a ship during the Korean War. The couple married on a Sunday afternoon. That night, he reported back to the Pennsylvania Navy Yard and his bride returned to Washington.

"After three months, I got pregnant," Wald recalled. "Eventually, I got around to telling my bosses. They were very good about it. I stayed until a month or so before the baby came and, by that time, two of my husband's three years of service were over and they gave him shore duty. So I moved to Norfolk and that's where I had the baby. We stayed until he was out the following December. Again, the firm was very good. They would have let me come back if I'd wanted to, but I didn't want to. I didn't plan anything. I just knew I wanted to stay home with my baby.

"My husband never pressured me to do that, it was what I wanted. I have a tendency, the kind of personality, that when I do something, I do it intensely. I really felt motherhood was that kind of an experience and I didn't want somebody else doing it for me."

Wald's mother worked and her three daughters currently combine children and careers: "I think this is a choice that some of us are allowed and others are not," she said. "In the back of my mind, I always believed I could go back to work when it was the right time."

For ten years, Wald stayed home. Three daughters and two sons were born within seven years, the last in 1960 when she was 32. Over the next few years, Wald worked at home. A friend writing a book on Robinson-Pattman price discrimination asked for her help with footnotes.

"When the kids napped," Wald recalled, "I'd run to the den and get out the typewriter. I also worked at night. What I wanted to do was build a little bit of experience to fill that 10-year gap."

Many family friends were lawyers which made it easier to keep up with developments in her field and to get work when she wanted it. One friend, Dan Freed, now a Yale professor, worked in the Robert Kennedy justice department. "Bobby Kennedy had become interested in the problems of poverty in the criminal justice field," Wald said, "and Dan was suddenly given the task of coming up with all this research and project development on poverty and the criminal justice system. This was in the early 1960s and he was all by himself. He managed to get funding for research and hired me.

"I'd go to his office, at most, two mornings a week when the cleaning woman came in to watch the kids. The first problem we worked on was bail and we wrote a book together called *Bail in the United States* (1964) which was the first publication I'd had.

"That led to doing a book (*Law and Poverty*: 1965) for the Legal Services program which was getting off the ground as part of the War on Poverty program under Sargent Shriver."

In 1965, Wald was appointed to the President's Commission on Crime in the District of Columbia. She became a consultant to the President's Commission on Law Enforcement and Administration of Criminal Justice a year later. From there she advanced, by appointment, to commissions on civil disorder and causes and prevention of violence.

"During this period," she said, "my kids were still in school and I was concentrating mainly on research writing—so that I could go out to do research and write at home. It was hectic, but I retained the notion I needed to be available if the kids needed me or somebody was sick that day."

By 1968, things had changed. Richard Nixon became president. Wald, a lifelong Democrat, had no GOP connections. With her children well-launched in school, she was ready to work, but uncertain of how and where to start.

"I remember being on a family vacation in August," she said. "It was 1968 and the time of the Democratic convention. We watched the riots in Chicago on TV. I'd just turned 40 and I thought, 'Oh, my god, it's over. What am I going to do? I don't have a practice. It's not likely that a law firm will take me in, based on all of the public policy stuff I've been doing for the last seven or eight years. Government jobs are unlikely to continue, so I won't be doing any consulting. What does the future hold?'

"So I did something which certainly had its risks and for a period of time was, well, humbling. I'd done all that research for the book on law and poverty, but I'd never done hands-on, so I went to the local Legal Services office and said, 'Here I am. Will you take me on? I don't know how to file a piece of paper or any of the kinds of things you do in actual practice, but I'll do anything you want me to.'

"Legal Services," Wald explained, "if not revolutionary, had in its early days the notion it would make big differences in the lives of poor people—class action suits, going after the bureaucracy.

"The traditional, old style Legal Aid was, basically, 'We'll do something for this person to get him out of the trouble he's in today.' That was necessary, but this new concept was, 'We'll challenge the regulations that keep people poor; We'll make big differences.'"

In one case, Wald worked on changing a District of Columbia regulation that required a woman who wanted a divorce but couldn't afford her own lawyer, to first deposit $100 with the clerk's office.

"If her husband had deserted her and she wanted to enter into a new marriage or start a new life, she couldn't if she were poor," Wald said. "It sounds ridiculous now, but it was the law. We challenged it and I argued it—in this court actually.

"A second challenge was to the so-called warrant of habitability. That meant that when a landlord rented an apartment, there was an implied warranty that the place was habitable. This got to the rat problem. We had people who refused to pay rent because rats were biting their children. We said, 'If you're going to hold yourself out as a landlord, it is implied you are renting something human beings can live in.' And that case also came before this court and was won."

Wald remained with Legal Services two years, then, in the 1970s, moved to what is called public interest law. She joined groups of lawyers working on the kinds of cases she'd been involved in with Legal Services, but in more specialized areas. Environmental and civil rights lawyers were in that category, as were lawyers working for the rights of women, the rights of the mentally ill, and of children. These were not lawyers for the government which, many times, was the opponent, but were attached to private foundations, for instance, the Sierra Club. Wald joined the Center for Law and Social Policy, one of the first such groups.

"Out of that came something called the Mental Health Law Project which is now the Bazelon Center for Mental Health Law," she said. "David Bazelon was a former chief judge of this court—very active and very liberal—whom I'd known through the 1960s and 70s. I and a couple of others were the founding people of the Mental Health Law Project and for five or six years brought test cases for the rights of the mentally ill and mentally retarded to needed services." One example was the Mills case in the District of Columbia, the second of its type in the United States. It claimed that under both local statute and the Constitution, retarded or mentally ill children had the right to schooling commensurate with their capabilities.

At that time, only one small program in the district enrolled retarded children or those with mental illnesses. When its capacity of a couple of hundred was reached, that was the end of it. There was nothing else.

"Our clients were 12- and 13-year-old children who'd received no education at all," Wald continued. "We brought a class action suit claiming they had a right to some form of education from which they could benefit. We won that case and it caused enormous uproar in the district because of the financial implications, but it began a much, much greater commitment to the education of handicapped children.

"The case here and a similar case in Pennsylvania became the basis on which Congress legislated the Education For All Children Act. I testified on our experiences at a Senate committee and eventually an act passed which gave federal funding to communities for the education of disabled children. It's been in operation ever since."

A second major case in which she was involved was the deinstitutionalization of those who suffer from mental illness and present no danger to themselves or others; who could, with some support and services, live within the community.

A suit was filed against the District of Columbia: Medical personnel would decide which individuals needed total institutionalization, which ones could be released to the community with appropriate support. The idea was to redirect money being spent on institutional buildings and personnel to community services.

"We won the lawsuit," Wald said, "but 20 years later, the money still hasn't been taken out of the empty beds and put into community services because of the political implications. Changes are opposed by those who work in institutions and need their jobs and by residents who object to community homes in their neighborhood. Some good has been done, but more could be done. The concept is right, but it's not easy.

"I ended up being head of the litigation section of the Mental Health Law Project and then the Carter administration came on and it was committed to having more women and minorities in government. I was appointed assistant attorney general for legislation in the Justice Department under Attorney General Griffin Bell, so for two and a half years, I did the department's legislative work. From there I was appointed to the bench in 1979."

Wald said the women's movement had very little effect on her life, though she supported it and marched in 1978 for passage of the Equal Rights Amendment. She believed she did benefit by the push to add more women to government.

She saw several steps as significant to her career: being channeled into college; getting a clerkship with Judge Frank; public policy research and writing in the 1960s which gave her credibility.

"A key year was 1968, when I decided I was not going to be just a person writing, but someone with hands-on experience," she recalled. "That led me to the area of test cases—using the law as an instrument in changing social policy. That's a controversial concept now, but not then.

"I think it was tremendously important to have gone to the Carter administration. Griffin Bell was very important in my getting this appointment. He was a close friend of President Carter and insisted he have a major hand in the appointment of judges. When he backed me, I believe that was a key step.

"I actually had a controversial confirmation, though there was nothing in my personal lifestyle, not anything like that. The far

Patricia McGowan Wald

right was then beginning to war up, and I had written several articles in the 1970s about the legal rights of children. That's why they attacked me—on the grounds of being anti-family and being against parental rights. I don't think my nomination was ever in any real danger, because it was a Democratic congress and a lot of people there knew me, but it was terribly uncomfortable to be attacked, not to be able to answer back, and worrying."

When Wald clerked for Judge Frank in a sister court to the one in which she now sits, she never imagined she'd be there as well.

"I knew it was a great job," she said, "and I suppose if someone had asked me, 'What job would you like?' I would have picked this one. But I really didn't have a game plan any more than I had an expectation I would make it."

She's now grateful she wasn't appointed until she was 50: "It's very worthwhile and I've enjoyed it, but judging is work in a restricted environment. You can't speak out, get out there and fight for causes," she explained.

"You have to be very careful to avoid publicity and can't even speak before advocacy groups. The fact that you have some power to wield is a good enough tradeoff, but I wouldn't have wanted that in my 30s. I really enjoyed my years of advocacy.

"Also, this is much more of an isolated job. You don't pick your colleagues. In the outside world, you tend to gravitate to people who share your values and your visions, who can share your projects. In the court, you come and then a new administration arrives on the scene and they appoint people with ideologies that are not at all the same. I find people now are coming from some place completely different than I, although you try to compromise your differences to the extent that you can do so.

"In this work, it's rare to have close friends. You spend a lot of time with people you may respect, but it's not like having a pal that you can let your hair down with because she shares your perspective. So you end up doing most of your professional work yourself and with your law clerks. Another thing about judging is you can't talk about it outside. You can't say, 'I've now got this interesting case. What do you think about it?' This is absolutely forbidden. You can't discuss it before or even afterward, and yet this is what your entire life is focused on. The only people you can talk to about this are your colleagues who don't talk much. And the law clerks are great, but they're kids and worried about their own careers and girlfriends."

What made the effort worthwhile? Money? Power? Ego?

"It's not salaries," Wald replied, "though I'm not complaining. We're now at $137,000 a year and that's fine, but there must be several hundred professions out there with people of commensurate talents and skills earning much more. It's not the money, not the prestige at this level. Ask an ordinary citizen to name any but possibly a Supreme Court justice, they won't have a clue. I suppose, ultimately, it's two things: One, the notion that you are working on things that matter. I'm not suggesting they matter as much as what the President is doing, what Congress is doing, or the more pro-active branches of government are doing.

"Still they are disputes which have meaning to the people and, very often in this court, not just to individuals but large groups of the populace. So there is the notion that you're spending your professional time on something that matters. "Second, and maybe an even more important aspect, is that you are your own person. Not the President, your colleagues who disagree with you, no one can tell you, even though you may be on a dissenting side, that you must adopt this point of view, that you may lose your job if you keep saying 'This is wrong' when everyone else is saying 'This is right.'

"You are allowed, within your own constraints, to say so if you think something is wrong or something is right. I'm not saying your colleagues can't out vote you, or the Supreme Court can't say 'No, you were wrong.' But it is your shot. I have contemporaries—and I'm in my mid-60s—who earn far more money than I do but can't make that statement."

At that time, a straightforward, no adjective, listing of Wald's work, related activities, publications, honors, and international activities filled eleven, single-spaced, typewritten pages. She served as chief judge of her court from 1986 until 1991. She's first vice-president of the American Law Institute and a fellow of the American Bar Association Foundation and the American Academy of Arts and Sciences.

Sixteen universities have awarded her honorary doctorates, among them Notre Dame, Colgate, Yale, Villanova, and Georgetown. Both the New York and Washington, D.C., women's bar associations gave her annual awards, as did the National Association of Women Judges in 1994.

Her publications have addressed criminal justice, juvenile law, mental disability, administrative, poverty, and constitutional laws, among others. She was a member of the first Canadian-American legal exchange; on the Salzburg faculty; led a judicial workshop for Czechoslovakian judges; was a participant in a U.S.-Russian seminar on environmental policy; consultant on the Lithuanian Constitution; delegate to Helsinki Accord meetings; and a participant in workshops and seminars in China and Scotland, as well as a dozen other locations.

But her work in Legal Services was what she took most pride in. Writing the book, *Bail in the United States*, with Freed had been a catalyst. "It seemed to open up the field," she said, "and I had a piece of action in getting the poverty and criminal justice program started. Changes would have come anyway, but I'm glad they came with my help.

"I've never fooled myself that the law is the answer to all problems," Wald continued. "In many cases, all the legal action can do is break a logjam, the same way that Brown vs the Board of Education ended legal segregation. Integration didn't happen immediately, and it still hasn't happened completely.

"It takes years and years for people to work out things at every level. But it's a starter process.

"I do think some of the work in the 1970s in the public interest areas—say, the right of the handicapped to education—really did make a difference. I know there are problems—what do you do about children with emotional problems in classrooms or the level of conditions for children sent to training schools—but I think that cases I worked on did change people's lives."

She may have written more dissents than the average judge. She recorded her disagreement with a majority of judges in the 1994 case of holocaust survivors' right to sue the German government for pensions and in the reversal of the Oliver North prosecution.

Dissents are important, she said, "Maybe these things won't change now, but at least I recorded my opinion that they should. Someday."

Wald and her husband live in a mid-town, Connecticut Avenue apartment. They enjoy a wide circle of friends. Both are movie buffs. Whenever she's free, Wald shows up for a noon hour jazzercize class at the courthouse. She walks the mile or so each way from the subway to the courthouse. An additional source of exercise and relaxation are six grandchildren.

Her work day begins at 8 a.m. and she usually works straight through until 6:30 or 7 p.m. She takes work home but seldom stays late at her office.

"That's the good thing about running your own shop," she said.

The formula, based on age and years on the bench, that determined when she can retire, had been satisfied and if she wanted to, she could walk out of her chambers forever or retain half of a regular work load and her offices. For the moment at least, she wasn't looking at either option, nor was her husband planning changes.

"We're smart enough to know we can't go on forever," she said, "and it could stop tomorrow. I guess we'll just adjust then. But as long as I'm able, I want to have some law-related outlet.

"I've been blessed, so far, with no major health impairments. My energy level is less and by the 11 o'clock news my eyes are closing. I realize, too, that there are some things I am never going to do, it's just too late. Like saying 'Maybe someday I'll do relief work in Somalia.' No, I won't. And I'm beginning to lose friends, people that were important in my life.

"The other thing that's sometimes hard about aging is looking back and watching things you worked very hard at and thought very important that are now eroded or—even worse—were transitory. Maybe we weren't always right.

"In the great scheme of things, it's hard to evaluate. In some cases, it's a tradeoff. You see you made one decision that led to a result that maybe you wish it hadn't.

"But nonetheless, you wouldn't have not made the decision because that also led to something you're glad about.

"Maybe on a second go-around, I would have tried to move into actual laying-on-of-hands practice earlier than I did. I've been a little hesitant to push myself. That may be a generational thing. I was willing to be a laborer in the vineyards. To some degree, in my early years, people took advantage of that. You do the work. Someone else takes the credit. I'm not at all sorry about the time I spent at home."

9

June Lee Biedler, researcher, former department head, Memorial Sloan-Kettering Cancer Center, New York City; member executive committee Sloan-Kettering Institute; born 1925; bachelor's Vassar; master's Columbia; Ph.D. Cornell.

I wandered to the top. I blundered to the top. I was focused on a goal of achievement. I was NOT focused on career advancement. I didn't know anything about it," June Biedler admitted at one point during the afternoon conversation. "But it worked out all right."

Listening to her, there seemed no doubt of her qualifications for a successful career in science. What seemed more remarkable was having a career at all, given the society she came from and the tenor of her time.

Biedler retired as head of the Laboratory of Cellular and Biochemical Genetics at Memorial Sloan-Kettering Cancer Center in New York City in the summer of 1994. During her years there, she made two major scientific findings: one resulted in new treatment approaches for cancer; the other furthered knowledge of tumor biology.

She talked about her scientific career and her life on a rainy day in Greenwich, Connecticut, in the house she shared with her friend, Gloria Heath.

"I began my life in New York City on eighty-something street," Biedler said. "Soon after I was born, my family moved to Rye, New York. Rye was a small, snobbish, closed community. My father was a Yale man. My mother hadn't gone to college. My parents divorced when I was about seven. My mother remarried. He was an investment banker and my best supporter in terms of being interested in me—who I was, what I did, and how I went about it. I was an only child and something of a bookworm.

"I became interested in science at Rye Country Day, a private school, because of Clinton Allen, a biology teacher. He told us about things in real life. Like, 'Where did the drinking water in New York City come from?' I asked him. 'Where did my shirt come from?' This was before synthetics, 'How did it get made?' And he told me. I could ask him anything and he was nice about it, didn't make me feel stupid at all. I said, 'Gee. I think science is wonderful. This is what I'd like to do.'

"The other day, I met a gal who said, 'Oh, you came from Rye. Did you go to Rye Country Day? Did you know someone called Clinton Allen?' And it turned out he'd done the same thing for her. He knew how things worked and I think that appeals to kids. Curiosity was part of it, and encouragement—being able to talk those things over.

"I then went away to Madeira, a private school outside of Washington, D.C. Pearl Harbor occurred when I was there.

"It was a girls' school and still is—enlightened, high scholastic standards. Madeira did a lot for me and I made many friends.

"I, and about 20 of my classmates, went on to Vassar. This was before the discovery of DNA and that meant science was at a peculiar turn. I decided I wanted to go to medical school. I didn't know about the existence of graduate school or that most of my professors had Ph.D's."

At Vassar, Biedler enrolled in pre-med courses and got a bad draw in roommates.

"The only way I could get through it was to avoid her," she recalled, "and the only way I could avoid her was to work during the night and sleep during the day. The result was I cut a lot of classes and got kicked out of Vassar.

"I hadn't asked anybody for advice. I didn't know enough to say, 'Look, I have this problem...' I was readmitted with the help of some faculty and student friends; Miss Madeira, who knew of my good academic record at her school; and my stepfather, who came up and pleaded my case with the dean. But it was a setback, and now I didn't have a very good scholastic record. I'd also become bored with classes that weren't well taught. I was spoiled by Madeira. The classes were big at Vassar, and you had to do whatever was dished out to you. I've never been able to do that. Easily turned off, I guess. Some courses were good, but not my science classes. And it was a bad time for science. No DNA: The genetic basis for how things work wasn't known then.

"Famous last words when I flunked out were: 'Your marks are so good in French, you should become a French major.'

"I told them I'd rather flunk out than major in French which was mostly reading novels."

Biedler grimaced: "Fun."

She was a pretty woman, small-boned and lean, with fine features. Often what she said was enhanced by well-timed shrugs and turns of head. Irony, her own, produced small smiles. Biedler had an endearing openness, a directness related to honesty. She said she hoped her stammering—infrequent—wouldn't bother us. It didn't bother her, she added.

"At Vassar," she continued, "the route was going to be, work a few years, then get married and that's that. So I finished up with a biology major and went to work for a guy in New York. He was at Memorial Sloan-Kettering Cancer Center and he recruited girls from Vassar because he knew they were well-educated, it wasn't far away, and it was a good thing to do: He might become friends with that person and eventually they'd marry. And he did, indeed, marry a Vassar classmate.

"I spent three years as a technician in the lab and cancer clinic, in hematology, and learned about drug resistance. Chemotherapy was new and it was interesting. At the time it was thought, 'This is the way to control and cure cancer. Surely a cure would come from these drugs.'

"Sloan-Kettering had just started and Alfred Sloan and Charles Kettering were around. The building wasn't even built when I started, so I was there from the beginning.

"The director, whom Mr. Sloan and Mr. Kettering hired, treated everyone very well and you got to know everybody and people weren't elitist at all, even if you didn't have an advanced degree. The air of optimism was real and during my early days there, the cure rate of one form of cancer—childhood leukemia—went from zero to 70 percent. People are discouraged now, but I was there when that happened, even though I wasn't doing it myself.

"I came into contact with patients, including children, and that was good for me. Being an only child, I hadn't had much contact with children and I learned lots of things.

"But I got very bored with work after three years and I thought I was going to marry. Those were the days when you went out and stayed up terribly late at parties, drinking and dancing, then went to work the next morning. I thought maybe if I stopped work, I'd be a nicer person. I did stop and I wasn't. So that fell apart. He was a dear person who went on to become an alcoholic. I didn't marry him, but I had that year when I didn't work. That didn't look good on my record.

"In those days, men would come back from World War II and I'd say, 'Why don't you do something worthwhile and useful, like teach, rather than sell insurance or Christmas tree ornaments?'

"The best answer I got was, 'Look. For three years I've been on a boat where the desk and chairs rocked and I want to sit behind a desk, in a comfortable chair, in an office that isn't rocking, and make a little money and get on with life and that's all I care about.'

"After that affair ended, I thought, 'June, you tell all these guys they ought to do this or they ought to do that, maybe you should be the one to do it?' So I got a job at American Optical Company and learned a lot but also learned I wasn't calling the shots.

"I obtained a master's degree—which as we all know is nothing much in higher education now. I went to Columbia which had really marvelous people—all of whom had their hand in and on DNA and genetics. This was 1954 and after I'd gotten out of Vassar in 1947 there'd been tremendous change. At Columbia, we had the prime geneticists, biologists, zoologists, in the U.S. and the world, as teachers.

"I'd backdoored my way into Columbia—a guy who thought he was in love with me, a graduate student there, had a good professor and he got him to say he'd give me a chance."

After earning a master's in zoology, Biedler moved to Rockefeller University as a technician in the laboratory of Rene Dubois, a Swiss famous for his work in tuberculosis.

"It was exciting," she said, "but you punched a time clock and they treated women technicians like two cents, so I knew I'd have to do something different with my life."

In 1954, after some hammering on the door, she was admitted into Cornell's graduate school for medical sciences' doctoral program.

Challenging studies didn't combine well with an active social life. One Saturday morning, six months into it, Biedler nursed a headache and fought exhaustion. Impending exams made everything worse. When the phone rang, she didn't answer it. Throughout the coming days she listened to periodic ringings and never picked up the phone. Even now she can't explain why, but on that date, her focus changed.

"I gave up everybody," she said. "I'd gone through some kind of awakening and was getting serious. I just didn't want to go out again until I got done what I wanted to get done. That worked. I'm glad I made that decision, and it was a deliberate one.

"After that, the kinds of people who said, 'Let's get married' were all in important positions like banking or something, and if I'd married, there was no way I could have gotten through graduate school because you have to devote your life to that. Every moment, really.

"I think at some point, if some guy had said, 'June, come away and live with me in Arabia,' I would have gone. But they said, 'What I want to do is work in Manhattan and then what I want is a chicken farm in upstate New York.'"

Doctoral studies proved more difficult than anything she'd ever done.

"Getting a Ph.D.," she recalled, "is highly unstructured and a fierce individual battle against people and things and subjects. And I had to overcome this very poor academic record and the indelible memory that Vassar had told me I was a bad student."

Her doctorate was in biology, cytogenetics, which is chromosome analysis, and at the time, suggested new approaches to cancer research. Study of chromosomal changes might unravel some of the mysteries of cancer.

Sloan-Kettering rehired her with the understanding that she would return to the center after a year—1959-1960—as exchange investigator at France's Institute Gustave-Roussy. "It's sort of a usual thing in the sciences to do a post-doc for a year," Biedler explained. "Usually you go to Europe if you're American. Having seen 'American in Paris' six times and having been there once on a post-college trip, I went to France. I took all of the clothes I'd need for a year. It's inconceivable now, but then it was a total separation. You didn't fly back for Christmas."

When her year was up, Biedler returned, as planned, to Memorial Sloan-Kettering Cancer Center. The center is both a cancer treatment facility—one of the three largest in the country—and a research center. It is perhaps a reflection of the effectiveness of the research to which Biedler contributed significantly that a 1994 survey called Sloan- Kettering number one for cancer treatment.[1]

During her years there, Biedler made two major scientific observations. A 1992 national award acknowledged her discovery of a key genetic mechanism and leadership "in the elucidation of the mechanisms by which mammalian cells develop resistance to cancer chemotherapeutic agents."[2] Biedler's work, according to her citation, resulted in new treatment approaches: By establishing a series of neuroblastoma cell lines, she'd been able to make fundamental observations in tumor biology.

At the time she made her findings, which she called the result of hard work and good luck, she'd had to sell them to the scientific community.

"In the case of both of my (published) observations, I was deliberately upstaged—by an American bastard and a Canadian bastard. But all of that made me much more competitive which is what I needed to be. What one does in science is to go to meetings, present data, write about it, talk about it, be visible. I got that way. For years, I'd only known that I liked what I was doing. I didn't know it was up to me to sell myself and march up the ladder.

"My stepfather, some years ago, had asked, 'June, where do you want to go? What do you want to attain?'

"'I don't know,' I said.

"He said, 'Come on, you have to know what position you want.'

"At the center, we call ourselves assistant members, associate members and members, which is the equivalent of assistant, associate and professor. So I told him, 'If I could just get halfway along—we had instructors then—become an associate member, I'd be very glad.' That was so dumb of me.

"It was a good question and the only time anyone had expressed an interest. My father was bewildered by my career and my mother was puzzled by it all. And nobody in Rye, New York—i.e., men— of my age went on and did anything other than investment banking or insurance or ever even moved away. Women, of course, married, had children, and became full-time homemakers."

June Lee Biedler

About a dozen years before Biedler left the center, a new CEO instituted tenure. Forty professional staff members, Biedler among them, were reviewed. "Even if you were a full member," she said, "if you didn't pass muster for tenure, you could be let go."

At that same time, the research effort divided into four programs, with cell biology and genetics one of these. "There was someone everyone expected would be chairman of the program and instead they picked me," Biedler said. "It was wonderful for me because it gave me a leadership position I'd not had before. I never thought that would happen and it happened.

"It made me change, broadened my outlook. I was then automatically a member of the 10-member executive committee of the Sloan-Kettering Institute. I was the only woman and it was the hardest time for me as a woman that I had experienced. I was just different. No one slapped my back or patted my shoulder when I came in the room. I'd known some of these guys quite well and everyone was very nice. But I was a loner, apart.

"I didn't have the opportunity for small talk—not to crack jokes and have fun—but to know a little bit about the others. I had to be brave to walk in. I would summon my courage and tell myself to calm down and shut up. For a little while I did a lot of stammering—more than usual, because I was plain nervous.

"All of us were busy chairing review committees. It was a terrible time because a lot of people were being asked to leave. I was actually glad to be one of the program chairmen because one was a real so-and-so and not kind to the people he was having to tell they no longer had more than a year or so at Sloan-Kettering.

"Some people can take it and some are nearly destroyed by that kind of information. I was glad I was handling my own people. Not that ultimately it was any better, but it was how it was done. For me that was a good experience. I knew I had some organizational and people skills, but they weren't being well used. This made me use them."

Papers Biedler had sent on before the interview included her talk at her retirement ceremony. She'd said then, "My first 20 years were filled with fear and the last 20 years with anxiety..."

For the last 30 years, she explained, she'd had to raise at least $300,000 a year in order to fund supplies for the laboratory, salaries for enough people to make the project go, and much of her own salary.

"Memorial only supplies you with a place," she continued. "They give you laboratory space. After that you raise your own operating funds. As my salary increased, I couldn't raise that much to cover it and so Sloan-Kettering provided about a third of it. They want you to have a certain amount of 'ungrant-supported' salary so that you are open to further grant support here and there.

"Funding is one big reason I quit a year early. My last grant was up July 30 of that year (1994). The projects had gone well, and I could have fought to renew. But my laboratory was getting smaller—the most people I ever had were ten—and my interest was less in telling people what to do....If you do that for a long period, it's wearying." Biedler's work had been with neuroblastoma, a cancer that affects the peripheral nerves of infants under the age of two and usually is fatal within two years. Because the disease is rare, funding through the United States system of National Institutes of Health grants had been difficult.

Researchers involved in breast or prostrate cancers, for instance, had an easier time with funding.

"The (scientific funding) situation is abominable," she said. "Democratic or Republican administration, doesn't matter. Money is curtailed. There's just less of it; the debt's bigger; certain voices say there shouldn't be basic research. Who in Congress understands basic research?

"In the natural sciences, we're the strongest nation in the world, but this is going down because we're not supporting as many young people starting out with, maybe, half-baked ideas. But that's how you begin. More monies are being delegated to specific areas, like breast cancer or AIDS. All these need money, but there isn't enough to go around. For awhile, there was so much money given to AIDS research that some of the work was of poor quality."

Her work is continuing at Fordham University with Bob Ross, a close colleague and collaborator, and his research assistant who worked with Biedler for 30 years, until her retirement.

"Fordham has appointed me Distinguished Research Scientist—without pay—in the Department of Biological Sciences and provided me with an office," she said. "All the cell lines developed at my lab are over there and I interact with them all the time. We write papers together, which makes life much more interesting and is also important because you need the input of more than one head.

"I expect I will go on for a few more years anyway," Biedler continued. "Actually, I can't see it ever ending, but I'm not so unrealistic as to think it goes on forever.

"Memories of the women's movement? Not too many, even though I recognized, just as I was getting my doctorate, that though it was a little tougher row to hoe if you were a woman, it really wasn't that tough if you worked hard. (Women) M.D.'s I knew had a tough time getting promoted and didn't have the peer help. But in science you're going it alone anyway.

"One reason I never engaged much during the women's movement is that I thought I wasn't a role model. It seems to me the women's movement was—and is—all about being a wife and mother and still doing what you wanted to do.

"In those days, most of the women and some of the men I knew didn't marry because of single mindedness. Few of my contemporaries (in science) married and a dull lot they are. No. I don't think I'm so dull. I don't mean to sound superior, but I had the advantages of an early social life and of a school (Madeira) and a liberal arts background which I think is tremendous.

"I was lucky, actually, to find Gloria as a friend. She was in New York City when I was at Sloan-Kettering. She was the only woman I knew who cared about work, too, and who was serious about it. I'd met her when I was at Vassar. We were both involved with playing lacrosse and running the U.S. Women's Lacrosse Association.

"Though I knew her then, I had a gang of friends and Gloria wasn't part of them. She was a loner."

Some years later, when each of them were living in New York, they had occasion to work together on lacrosse association matters. One project was a newsletter.

"Gloria knew how to do these things and had an office in New York where we could work on them," Biedler said. "It just turned out we got such things done with no difficulty. And, after a while, we'd get together once a month for dinner and it was fun. And Gloria was serious. I don't mean she was without humor and laughter. Quite the reverse. She was a good sport and I inveigled her to type my thesis and hold mice for me when I needed someone to help on weekends or Christmas Day. She hated it, but she did it. Then this other business with her house, my building on to it, just evolved." Biedler's part of the house was self-contained with a two-story living room and fireplace, a loft above for a work area, and bedroom over the garage. The living areas featured many Escher paintings which Biedler had bought in Amsterdam and family heirlooms of Far Eastern furniture.

Biedler said she'd slept in that morning and usually did. "Except for Saturday and Sunday, I got up and went to work every single day of my life," she said.

"I never took more than one or two weeks vacation since 1954, unless I include that year in France. That's one reason I quit early. That sense of 'Why can't I sleep in the morning?'

"Though I seem calm, I'm not. I do a lot of outdoors work and that helps, but I need nine hours sleep."

Biedler retains active membership in many different science-related societies and just completed a two-year term on the board of the American Association for Cancer Research. She still serves on the editorial boards of a number of scientific journals.

She'd used reading, groundskeeping, and sports as releases from the tensions of work and thought when she retired, she'd read more, but admitted she hasn't gotten past page 15 of anything.

"I do hope to wind down a bit," Biedler said, "get more efficient, conquer these huge masses of paper that still fill three, five-drawer files in my New York apartment."

Thinking of her life in general terms, she said she was most proud of "having learned, by working at it, to be a reasonably happy, uncomplaining person."

Of her scientific achievements, "I made two observations, major observations, that panned out to be important. I'm excited that I saw and made the interpretations—never mind the credit, it's having had the imagination to see and interpret the findings. It's knowing that it came right from my head. I did it.

"Without my eyes and my mind (these discoveries) would not exist, at least for a lot of years."

1 U.S. News and World Report: July 18, 1994.
2 Introduction at presentation of the Clowes Memorial Award to Biedler at the 1992 annual meeting of the American Association for Cancer Research.

10

Caroline Herzenberg, physicist, emergency
systems group, Argonne National Laboratory; born 1932; principal investigator Apollo
returned lunar sample analysis; Ph.D. University of Chicago; honorary doctor of science
State University of New York; producer, director TV science series.

Argonne Laboratory turned out to be a half-hour drive south-
west of Chicago. Whether or not Argonne was a town as
well as an institution wasn't apparent to a casual visitor.
Following Caroline Herzenberg's map and directions, we turned
at a two- to three-acre construction site and into a blacktop parking lot in front of a rectangular building of native concrete. The
building going up already looked like a twin. The only windows
in sight faced the parking lot. Inside, the dominant feature in the
large lobby was a counter arrangement, backed against the rear
wall and facing the door. There women signed us in and issued
clip-on badges, pointed the way to the restrooms and phoned
Herzenberg to come get us.

Herzenberg was slim, compact, perhaps 5-foot, 3- or 4- inches;
her skin was a redhead's; a platinum strip, from the crown to the
end of her bangs, highlighted auburn hair, cropped short. Her
glasses were amber-tinted. The burnt orange blouse tied at the neck

and was worn above dark slacks and under an orange-gold checked jacket.

We'd stood by for an earlier flight so the conference room she'd signed up for wasn't available. She took us instead to a small room adjacent to the employees lunchroom.

Herzenberg is a physicist with daunting credentials. Her resume listed her as physicist and emergency/energy systems engineer; Decision and Information Sciences division/Argonne National Laboratory. Argonne is a Department of Energy think tank, established after World War II, with about 3,000 to 4,000 employees.

Herzenberg earned her bachelor of science degree in physics from the Massachusetts Institute of Technology in 1953 and post graduate degrees from the University of Chicago in 1955 and 1958. At the moment, she was not doing mainline physics.

"Right now," she said, "I'm working in emergency preparedness—that's radiological emergencies at nuclear power plants. I've also been doing a little work on chemical stockpile and chemical weapon emergencies; a course of instruction and a little work with the Department of Energy on emergency systems for DOE sites—a problem with a nuclear reactor, for instance."

Even to a non-scientist, the questions sounded embarrassingly elementary.

"No," she said, "it's not all mind work; There's a fair amount of legwork required since we work with all of the states, some companies, and agencies and organizations."

She beckoned to a colleague at the food and drink dispensers outside and asked her to help fill in the blanks. The newcomer said there had been an emergency preparedness program since the reactor problem at Three Mile Island. Initially, Argonne became involved by providing evaluation and methodology and then by employing experts to assess emergency preparedness capabilities in state and local jurisdictions.

When the colleague left, Herzenberg, by request, started at the beginning: born in March 1932 in East Orange, New Jersey; Caroline Dorothea and Charles Frederick Littlejohn's only child.

I Can't Do What?

The family moved to Oklahoma when Caroline was 3 1/2-years-old; she went through the Oklahoma City schools system.

An overwhelming condition of her childhood had been her father's illness. A Spanish-American and World War I veteran, he came home to start a successful import-export business. When the Depression wiped that out, he failed as well. From then on, he divided his time between his home and veterans' hospitals, either recovering from or being treated for physical and mental illnesses. His daughter's most vivid childhood memory was coming upon his unconscious body on the floor. Though he'd suffered from a stroke, she believed him to be dead.

Caroline's mother wasn't typical of her time. She forbade dolls but allowed her daughter to play with toy soldiers and toy guns. She encouraged scholastic achievement though Caroline's school career began badly. She flunked kindergarten. How could you flunk kindergarten? Herzenberg believed it happened because she couldn't skip rope, identify all the colors, and didn't socialize to school standards. Later on she made up for it—skipping more than enough grades to catch up.

"I had some good teachers," she recalled. "Some of them seemed to me the most wonderful people in the world. We moved often and I didn't have many friends. I read a lot and I liked animals, but we lived in town so we couldn't have pets. My father was into hunting and fishing, though, so I got outdoors with him."

On one of her dad's duck hunting trips, she met Jimmy Norman, an entomologist doing field work at the lake. It was Norman who encouraged her aptitude for and interest in science.

The next major factor, in terms of influencing her future, resulted from a summer camp. There she chanced upon information about the Westinghouse Science Talent Search. She talked her teacher into letting her enter the competition during her senior year. "My display project was a collection of insects," Herzenberg recalled. "That I won was totally amazing. I think it's really great for kids to get breaks like this now and then."

During high school and college, she'd nothing specific in mind in terms of a career, just a vague image of herself as a solitary figure in a laboratory—a modern day Madame Curie with the details blurred.

One of her fellow students at the University of Chicago was Leonardo Herzenberg. The son of a mineralogist, he'd grown up in Bolivia and lived abroad all of his life. They married in July of 1961. Their elder daughter was born in 1965, the younger in 1979, when her mother was 47.

Two careers complicated their life together. Her husband, a computer engineer, worked most recently in Freeport, Illinois, about 125 miles north and west of Chicago. He lived there while his wife had an apartment in Chicago, nearer her job.

"Until he retired about a year ago and came here, we were always someplace different—except for brief intervals when I was without a job," said Herzenberg. "It's hard, as many people have found out, for two people who are professionally active, to find suitable jobs for each of them in a single location. We spent a lot of time commuting."

Herzenberg's first year after receiving her Ph.D. in 1958 was much as she'd imagined as a child—at the University of Chicago doing pioneering research on light heavy-ion studies. A year later, she came to Argonne for the first time—staying two years to do experimental low-energy nuclear physics and pioneering work on the Mossbauer effect.

A major career step moved her to the Illinois Institute of Technology as an assistant professor of physics. She arrived in 1961, stayed six years and left when she was denied tenure.

"There was a glass ceiling for women then and it still exists," Herzenberg said. "I was considered less desirable because I was a woman. For example, I found out my salary at IIT was next to the lowest of the entire faculty. Sure, I was disgusted, but I wasn't much of an activist."

She became one when she didn't get tenure at IIT. "I'm not sure why I didn't—probably a lot of reasons. I didn't go back and do heartfelt talks with everyone, and I'm not sure I would have gotten the answer if I'd done so. Another woman came onto the physics faculty after me and didn't get tenure either. In part, I think again it had to do with being a woman. I think they'd been interested in hiring someone inexpensive to take over from an IIT physics faculty member who'd had to leave suddenly—rumored to have been for some serious sexual improprieties. So there was this vacancy for someone in experimental nuclear physics and I assumed responsibility for his laboratory, classes, students and what not. I'm not an exceptional teacher, but I thought I was doing OK, so it was a very big shock to me when I didn't get tenure. If your road plan is to become a Marie Curie and you don't get tenure that's a difficult situation to face.

"Oh, I knew political antagonisms existed here and there, but I was at least an average tenure track faculty member and assumed I'd be promoted like everybody else."

When she wasn't, she slipped into serious depression that temporarily immobilized her. What made her situation worse, was the contract she'd won from the National Aeronautics and Space Administration as principal investigator of lunar rocks with applications of Mossbauer spectrometry.

In simple terms, the use of Mossbauer spectrometry allowed Herzenberg to analyze, without physical or chemical damage, the rocks brought back by Apollo astronauts:

"If you had a rock composed of a combination of minerals," she explained, "you were able to determine the different minerals present by shining gamma rays on the rock, without having to split it, or dissolve it, in order to analyze it chemically. And you can work with very small rock or soil samples."

The problem of where to conduct this research that NASA had selected her to do, without a laboratory, was finally resolved after she engaged an attorney. Believing her right to tenure had been denied because of her sex, she initially went to the American Civil Liberties Union. They declined to take her case, but recom-

Caroline Herzenberg

mended an attorney with a record of civil rights cases. He eventually negotiated a site for her research.

She moved from IIT to the IIT Research Institute, also in Chicago, and remained there from 1967 until her work was completed in 1971.

Rocks from the moon, she said, didn't look so different from those common to earth. Herzenberg worked with 20 to 30 samples; some were rocks the size of the end of her thumb, others lunar soil particles.

Until 1977 Herzenberg divided her time between unemployment and temporary teaching posts at the University of Illinois Medical Center and California State University at Fresno.

She enlivened those solitary periods with special interests. "The appointment at Fresno was temporary, for a year, so my family wasn't there and I had time left over," Herzenberg said. "As it happened the apartment building I was living in was at one end of an airport runway, so I ended up getting my pilot's license. It's a real expensive hobby. One of these days, if I have time and money—if I ever get rich, as unlikely as that seems—I'll have my own plane."

Another interim activity was judo. "I did that and some karate and aikido. But after my younger daughter was born, being effectively a single mother because my husband worked somewhere else, well, I didn't have much time for avocations anymore."

Since 1977, she'd been associated with Argonne. Professional interests had taken her to conferences in Israel and Australia, but her frequent trips were mostly within the continental United States. Coming up would be Logan, Utah, where she'd lecture at Utah State University on women scientists in the Manhattan Project. She and a colleague were collaborating on a book about it.

When she's at Argonne, a typical day begins at 5 a.m.: "I live in Chicago and I'm slow and tend to spend time in the shower. I eat breakfast, organize my life at home, and usually get here at 7:30. The first thing I do, is look at the E-mail. There's always lots of it—mostly from colleagues in physics, people with whom I have professional activities, and I'm secretary-treasurer of Forum on Physics and Society of the American Physical Society. After that, any mail or voice mail. That's all activity I need to take care of before I can get fully started here at the lab which is ordinarily about 8:30 or 9.

"I generally leave work about 5:15, get home about 6. My husband, the family hero, usually fixes dinner. Then there's dishes, laundry. I try to do a little reading—see what the kid's up to, help with her homework. Bed early. I'm not one of these people who can get by on five hours of sleep, but I could sure get more done if I were.

"My days really aren't that similar to each other, but when I'm here, that's an example. The work at the lab could typically be reviewing a radiological preparedness plan.

"There's a lot of travel. Coming up is a radiological emergency exercise at Three Mile Island, and I'll be there, along with a lot of other folks, for a week. A simulated emergency at TMI will let us watch how the emergency plays out, find out what the problems are in the state and local emergency responses, write reports."

Herzenberg's professional record includes lengthy lists of honors, board and committee memberships, professional affiliations and activities, and 10 pages, single-spaced, of published writings—books, articles, reports, and speeches to professional gatherings. She's an advisor for a Seattle-based, Public Broadcasting System-produced, TV science series, "Bill Nye the Science Guy," and produced and directed her own cable TV series, "Camera on Science."

She's also produced controversy. Her colleague had noted that, non-specifically, and writings about her referred to questions she raised during development of the Strategic Defense Initiative.

"Back in 1985, the SDI office needed a body," she said. "It was suggested that, since I was expendable, I should look into this. I went to Washington and sort of informally interviewed—'Is this person going to work out?'

"This person sure didn't work out. But in doing my homework, I got interested in the subject and pursued it to some extent on my own when I got back."

The resulting controversy came when Herzenberg pointed out that some of the lasers they planned to develop could be used for offensive as well as defensive purposes.

"Basically," she explained, "instead of shining the space-based lasers at enemy missiles, the lasers could be rotated toward targets on earth and used as incendiary weapons. What I was interested in particularly was the possibility of creating firestorms.

"I thought this was an important thing and people ought to know about it. So I wrote it up and sent it to the British journal, Nature. They were interested and held on to it for a long time but didn't publish it. I never figured out why except there might have been some concern about the British official secrets act. I did publish it eventually in a technical newsletter and then newspapers all over the world picked up the information. Unfortunately, I've not been popular here since. Having a staff member whose studies showed the capability of offensive use of the SDI and whose studies were reported in the newspapers was not good for local efforts directed toward getting money from the SDI office."

She admitted to being "in the doghouse a lot" but declined to talk about other such incidents.

"Major mistakes," she repeated. "An interesting question. Usually when people respond to that question, they give a diversionary answer. I probably will too. I've thought about that. Particularly in cases of women in science, to try to assemble a picture from just that question."

In her own case, she believed in retrospect she'd erred in turning down the opportunity to be acting chair of the physics department at Illinois Institute of Technology during a summer absence of the incumbent.

"No thank you," she said. "I wanted to teach and conduct research. I wasn't much interested in administration, not realizing that one of experienced scientists' functions these days—anywhere—is to get heavily involved in the management and administration of science. I've continued to be a contrarian in that area—not taking management responsibility—and that's unfortunate. I think I could have accomplished more if I'd just accepted this as a given—an activity I should have allocated some of my time to."

The project she enjoyed most was the lunar sample analysis: "It was a thrill, a high point, to hold a piece of the moon in my hands. You combine the objective with a kind of mythic quality."

Even if rocks were brought back from future space explorations, Herzenberg doubted she would have the opportunity to do this research again.

"I haven't done Mossbauer spectrometry in years and I don't have the equipment," she explained. "That's one of the problems if you don't have tenure. You move from place to place and you can't take it with you. You start all over again—without continuity and without graduate students. You must be at a place for a reasonable length of time so that your graduate students have some assurance they can conduct their thesis research and complete their degrees. I moved from job to job and I reset up Mossbauer spectrometry equipment several times and, finally, I simply gave it up. Jumping from job to job was very difficult emotionally, too, and I found it hard to do anything constructive during that time. It's just hard to pick yourself up by your bootstraps."

Her plans are to stay at Argonne as long as she's able to. There may be some pressures on employees to retire. She likes doing technical work and enjoys the environment. When she does retire, she hopes she and her husband will be able to afford to remain in Chicago where they just arranged a mortgage on a condominium.

"I like Chicago," she said, "but wherever I am, I want to be near a major library and a university and I'll probably spend a lot of time writing nasty letters to the editor."

Was she finding aging difficult?

"It's shit," she replied with a grin. "One function after another goes. I just got a hearing aid and it squeals when I try to adjust it. It never works right and I still haven't figured it out. Getting old is just no fun: in principle, no problem; in practice, a pain."

We followed her down the featureless halls, trotting to keep up. You could easily get lost because each long corridor looked exactly like the last—an occasional open door revealing a tiny, windowless cell. So much for the expenditures of taxpayers' money on frills and flourishes. None was evident here.

Herzenberg had been right when she said we'd meet in the lunch room because her office couldn't hold us all. I stood at the doorway while she slid sideways to get behind her desk. Fraser hovered between us with a camera. Floor to ceiling steel shelving filled with books and pamphlets opposite the door turned the corner and continued across the wall behind her desk. Because of papers on top of her desk, on the sides, and tilting from what must have been an upright section at the back, the desk configuration remained a puzzle: On the side farthest from the door, a lighted computer screen and a bit of a printer showed.

At an eye-level shelf by the door, a bumper sticker had been pasted: "Another environmentalist for nuclear power." Taped to the shelf above it, a Sunday comic of Shoe: subject, art and commentary of a desk and office that looked very much like Herzenberg's.

I asked about her professional goal at this stage of her career: "Before I die," she said, "I really want to understand how the universe works. I don't expect that will happen, but I'd like to do a little on it anyway."

11

Gloria W. Heath, aerospace scientist, consultant; born 1922; Smith College graduate; flew
with WASPS in World War II; committee
chair of International Academy of Astronautics; lifelong activist in space and air safety.

Gloria Heath, a pilot since her college days, has been deeply
involved in development of air then space safety ever since.
Those who work with her describe her as an initiator and
praise her insights and breakthrough thinking. She's spent a lifetime using those skills to make flight safer.

We had arranged to meet Heath, between her overseas trips,
in Greenwich, Connecticut, where she lived. We'd spent the night
in Greenwich, at a historical home turned into a bed and breakfast.
The following morning, we waited for her in a waiting cum living
room furnished with early 19th century chairs, tables and paintings. Across the street, cars parked along the circular drive of the
Greenwich Woman's Club, a one-time private residence that looked
well-kept, but a bit stodgy—like the 60-something matrons of the
forties and fifties. The last women's club building I remembered
seeing was years ago, in Grand Rapids, Michigan, where I grew
up. There must have been some morning function for the Greenwich women and what was it? In the mid-90s, what did members
of women's clubs do?

On time, Gloria Heath drove up in a Jeep-type vehicle, made the long step out of it without effort. A lean, limber, casually dressed woman, she moved quickly and, as was soon evident, talked at the same pace. She smiled often. Her hair was white. She wore the tailored, quiet clothes I associated with Eastern seaboard women.

"It's nice of you to offer to get to my house on your own," she'd said earlier on the phone, "but people always get lost and then aren't easily found." We followed her through winding streets and around corners in the built-up, central section of Greenwich and then slalomed through gates on alternate sides of streets past very large houses on landscaped grounds, set a long way back from the curb.

After a couple of miles, she turned into a long drive and parked outside an unpretentious, gray, clapboard house. The lot was large and wooded, with slopes and beds of greenery hiding the famous neighbors she'd mentioned. We'd parked at the rear of the house. The pillared front bordered Long Island Sound. Even on that gray morning, at low tide, a water view had great appeal.

Inside, an entry hall opened into a long living room furnished with large-scale, solid pieces. A door off the hall led to a cozy, wood-paneled room where, Heath said, most of the living went on. We followed her through a kitchen and narrow rooms without specific identity to the wing of the house where her friend, Dr. June Biedler, lived.

After stopping for a brief meeting with Biedler in a dining area, it was agreed to stay there. A glass wall faced the Sound and a nice sound of rain underscored the conversation.

Heath saw the earth from an airplane window for the first time when she was a freshman at Smith College. Her only brother, older, in flight training at university, had talked his instructor into taking her up. That one brief flight set the course for Heath's future.

Her first step was to organize a flying club at Smith. "Then," she recalled, "I got the trustees at Smith to allow us to buy an airplane. We each had a $100 share in a $1,500 airplane. We hired our own instructor and paid $3 an hour for instruction. When you graduated, you sold your share."

She'd recalled that early involvement when she spoke at Smith's 1994 class day ceremonies. The plane, she told students and alumna, had been bought just a year after the United States entered World War II. At a christening ceremony for the plane, the speaker noted that from the cockpit of airplanes, national borders and other symbols of territoriality were not perceivable.

From the very beginning, that had been the perspective of the world that so entranced, so drew Heath to the air: a pilot saw the earth as a continuum. "I was taken by everything about it," she said the morning of the interview, "It was during the war and the promise was that afterwards, nations would work together and the airplane would be a way of drawing people together."

At college, when she began flying, she wrote in her diary, "The view back on earth from the airplane was a peaceful one, anxieties seemed to melt away. The area in which the college was looked very small, though when I was down there, it was a big worry."

"And of course," Heath said, "when the space program came along, there was that view back to earth and what this had to do with man's future. I concluded that...unless we were in this together, (the world) would be a mess—selfish national interests would work against the cooperation necessary for only peaceful uses of space."

Heath was born in New York City and grew up on Long Island. Her father was a member of the New York Stock Exchange. Her mother, she said, had an artistic background which was never expressed. Educated at private schools, the one Heath talked about was Putney where she took summer programs from the age of 12 and then her senior year of high school. Founded by a pioneer in education, the Vermont school stressed responsibility. Summers, Heath said, "I did a little carpentry, apprenticed with the resident blacksmith, but mostly I herded cows. The cows always got into the corn which was way above my head so there was always this frustrating defeat by the cows.

"At that time I was not aware of the educational outlook, only its effect on daily life. If there was something you wanted to do, it would not be presented to you with other people having done most of the work. It was a total experience. If there was a play you'd agreed to put on, you'd have to do the whole of it—create the scenery and costumes yourself, hire a hall and sell the tickets.

"I graduated from Putney in 1939—after a college prep course, but college wasn't presented as the objective. You pursued as much of the studies at as good a pace as you could. If you were advanced, teachers responded to that. In your senior year, when college entrance exams reared their heads, you were told about them, multiple choices, whatever. We looked at the subjects, were told how to prepare ourselves, though we never got any drilling. 'Be sure to get plenty of rest,' I remember a teacher telling us. 'Don't work yourself into a frenzy. Remember, the exam cannot tell the difference between sleepiness and stupidity.'

"I think what I got from Putney was (confidence) to pursue objectives on my own and probably an interest in how it all came about. And independence. I figured things out on my own. And I never, ever, thought if there was something I wanted to do, there was a reason not to try to do it."

She'd headed to Smith with no idea of what she wanted to do with her life. "My parents never channeled me. They had implanted in us, shored up, the idea of freedom. I never felt there were barriers, though maybe I was not sensitive.

"I was a very deliberate child. At Putney, I remember my English teacher asked me, 'Don't you ever have a day when you forgot whether you'd brushed your teeth?' I said, 'Oh no. I would know I brushed my teeth because I set out to brush them.'"

So it was at Smith, in the spring of her freshman year, when her brother arranged a flight for his younger sister. "I adored and admired and looked up to my brother," she said. "He was very kind to me, though he was very much more debonair." Heath paused. "He was a Renaissance man: He'd studied ancient Greek and Latin, but he was a wonderful bon vivant who took joy in living and things that brought joy, particularly people. He was very outgoing, very happy, and I was none of those things which is why I was so pleased he'd do things with me. He was a wonderful brother to take this not-so-attractive sister and it never occurred to him not to include me."

After graduating from Smith, she earned an instructor's rating and planned to teach in the Navy. "I thought this would be less of a vagabond thing to do," Heath said, "but my brother called me—he was in the Air Force—and said, 'No, no. Don't be silly. Join the WASPs. This is the future.' And of course he was right."

She signed up as a Woman's Air Force Service Pilot, or WASP. From 1942 until 1944, the Army Air Forces trained 1,830 WASPS picked from 25,000 applicants. Only 1,074 earned wings.

Jacqueline Cochran, first woman to break the sound barrier, was director. The idea was that the women, who wore uniforms but retained civilian status, would ferry planes and tow gunnery targets to free men for duty overseas. Heath flew a stripped-down, B-26 out of Pocatello, Idaho, the only woman in the tow squadron. The B-26, Heath said, came with a terrible reputation because of an extremely short wing. The entire operation was risky.

"We would go up to what seemed then like very high altitudes, 6,000 feet, and unroll this sleeve target and the P-47's would aim at it." Each fighter plane was equipped with automatic machine guns with live ammunition dipped in an identifying color. On-board cameras recorded strikes. "When we landed," Heath said, "the fighter pilots dashed to see how many hits they'd made while we rushed to see if our plane was in their film." Friendly fire often came uncomfortably close.

She, like all surviving WASPS—38 died in crashes—were officially out by December 20, 1944. It wasn't that women pilots hadn't worked out. They could and did fly any aircraft males flew. But as the war wound down and more men became available, women became the first to go.

"After I got out, I still wanted to do something in flying," Heath said. "I couldn't actually fly because that was very closed (to women) then, so I applied at Aero Insurance Underwriters. 'You've had this flying club experience,' the man who interviewed me said, 'and we'd like you to handle our flying clubs, but we can't pay you very much.'"

She accepted what was offered and worked on safety as related to loss prevention. One of the individuals who walked into her office was the inventor of the stall warning indicator. He'd devised a vane on the wing which sensed airflow loss and hooked that up to an audible warning in the cockpit. Indeed yes, insurance companies would lower premiums if plane owners installed the device. Another visitor brought an idea for a flight simulator to train corporate pilots like himself.

Because of her expertise and background, Heath became a founding member of the Flight Safety Foundation in 1948. The foundation was funded and founded by Laurance Rockefeller, then owner of Eastern Airlines. The idea was to disseminate safety information to foundation members who represented airlines and aircraft manufacturers. By pooling all reports of incidents, incipient accidents, FSF could correlate and analyze the information then pass that on to members.

"The reason you're interested," said Heath, "is that accidents are few, but incidents are many. You get an accident because various things have gone wrong, usually many, so the more incidents reported, the more you learn and can pass along to those new to the type of aircraft."

In the late 1940s, many countries, newly acquainted with advanced performance aircraft, set about establishing and operating national airlines. A vast spread existed between what these newcomers knew and flight technology and practices elsewhere.

The International Civil Aviation Organization formed to bring about some common standards for operations and training. Flight Safety and Heath fed them relevant information to make decisions. For instance, would altitude be reported in metric or "English"

Gloria W. Heath

figures? How could pilots who spoke different languages and dialects be understood among themselves, by air traffic controllers?

From the late 1940s to the mid-1960s, one of Heath's responsibilities at FSF became planning of international safety seminars with aviation agencies in countries outside the United States. She worked on procedures for emergency landings on water, a new concern. Before World War II, transoceanic aircraft were seaplanes. Postwar travel would be by land planes, most likely to be flown by military pilots. Heath, through FSF, found resources to test models of new aircraft that were to fly ocean routes.

She sought out experienced over-water pilots and promoted training sessions for transoceanic pilots. Another aspect of her work involved rescue of downed aircraft by ships. Heath prepared manuals to aid captains if they responded to a ditching. FSF also ran an accident investigation school which she established.

It was during these years that her brother died in an airplane crash.

"He was a marvelous pilot," she said. "He knew his aircraft and could take it way beyond recommended extremes. He knew what he could do and he liked the adventure. He flew fighters in the China, India and Burma theater and after the war, he came back and started an import-export business. He'd bought an airplane for his business and was flying from Wilmington on a routine flight. He was near Baltimore when an unforecast, occluded thunderstorm occurred.

"If you were flying, you'd see a few low clouds, but you wouldn't know there was a thunderstorm above you. He got caught in a terrific downdraft and realized he'd have to make a forced landing. There were houses all around. In order to avoid them, he picked what was not the best place to bring the plane down. He hit the trees and was killed. He was 28 when he died."

In 1961, Heath organized her own company, SAR-ASSIST Inc., consultants on flight safety, search, rescue, and survival, and makers of survival equipment. Through her recommendations and follow-up efforts, underwater acoustic locators attached to flight recorders became mandatory on commercial aircraft.

The advent of space flight in the late 1950s launched Heath on another challenge. She made the leap by becoming chairman of the International Academy of Astronautics' committee on safety and rescue. "The person who asked me to help knew of the work I'd done in aviation and rescue and said, 'Why don't you think about space?'

"I asked many questions and wrote voraciously. When someone asked about these things, they'd be told, 'You'd better talk to her.' I've always been a generalist and not a specialist," Heath continued.

Sufficient financial resources allowed her the freedom of working independently. "I wasn't hired by our space agency and wasn't working in an engineering plant. I wrote papers on my own for about 10 years, Survey of Space Recovery Capabilities."

Heath's voice registered her excitement: "I could see easily what was needed. There is a big lesson one learns: If you are responding to an astronaut's emergency landing site, not, of course, known in advance, you would not be able to have a dedicated force—trained personnel, ships, aircraft, whatever. Emergencies are too infrequent and stand-by dedicated forces too costly. What you have are non-dedicated forces and the way you do that is to know where all the trained people, all the necessary vehicles and equipment, are throughout the world. You'd have this information in a rescue coordination center and since this is a global viewpoint, we all help each other. That kind of global response could respond to astronaut emergency landings, as well as its present use to respond to individuals in distress on land or at sea. And satellites orbiting earth could aid those at risk in natural disasters.

"I was excited by the possibilities," she said. "Actually it was a passion." Heath had followed this passion ever since through her work with the International Academy of Astronautics, founded in 1960.

Similar to a National Academy of Science, scientists, engineers and lawyers involved with space are elected to membership by their peers. An official 1995 academy publication reported a thousand members from 65 countries and identified itself as a scientific institution devoted to fostering development of astronautics for peaceful purposes.

Various committees organize seminars, symposia, at annual International Astronautical congresses. Heath's initial contribution was co-authoring the Survey of (Space) Rescue Capabilities in 1968, the year the Safety and Rescue Committee formed. She was named committee chairman at the 1978 congress and served until 1989 when she continued as co-chairman. As chairman, she instituted a change of outlook, from a space-only interest to the benefits from space to life on earth. This became a major theme of future congresses. Her particular focus involved worldwide distress and disaster responses using earth-orbiting satellites for information.

Heath is a member of the Space Agency Forum, a coalition of space agencies such as the National Aeronautics and Space

Agency and its counterparts in other countries. Its focus is disaster prevention and response.

"My involvement was intense," she said. That effort was officially recognized by the IAA in late 1990 when she was presented with the IAA's Engineering Sciences Award "for significant and lasting contributions to the advancement of the astronautical sciences."

Heath stopped flying when she bought her house on Long Island Sound in 1964. She couldn't afford the house and the hours in the air necessary to keep up her commercial license. "If you fly," she said, "you ought to fly a lot, otherwise you're at a bit of a risk." She never married. "I did think about it. Looking back, I would say I could never have developed as I have—for better or worse—if I'd been married."

For most of her working life, she'd been the only woman in whatever it was she was doing, at any gathering she attended. Had she encountered discrimination? "I perhaps might not have perceived prejudice," she replied.

When she was elected to membership in the International Academy of Astronautics, there were seven other women members. A 1973 press release from the IAA reported two from the United States, Heath and Jacqueline Cochran, the former director of the WASPS. Cochran, an honorary member, did not become involved in IAA space activities, Heath said. Heath did recall what being a speaker at a Wings Club meeting involved. Wings Club members, all men, were international stars in the aviation field—presidents of airlines, aircraft manufacturers, owners of cargo companies.

Once a year, on Valentine's Day, they invited their secretaries to join them at the club for lunch. Then involved with the Flight Safety Foundation, Heath was invited—the first woman so recognized—to speak at a Valentine's Day luncheon. "I knew what I wanted to say," Heath said, "but I remember being coached: I was to talk about the foundation, its programs, what would interest members from their point of view. I was cautioned however, that I must not TELL them anything. If I was to even come out with a fact, I must preface it with 'As you already know...'"

Her activities on behalf of air and space safety continue. At a fall 1995 symposium on safety and rescue, Heath and H. Sax of Germany coordinated six sessions which featured 43 speakers from throughout the world—France, Germany, the Ukraine, the United States, and China.

What in her lifelong commitment to flight safety was she proudest of? The "intellectual satisfaction, as the result of curiosity, of being at the forefront—where you've placed yourself—because you think there are ideas not being pursued that should be pursued and making those ideas into reality."

At that point in her life, Heath was content in Greenwich because of its proximity to music, theater, and art and because of the natural beauty of her particular location. She traveled a great deal; had just returned from Jerusalem, before that Paris, would return to Paris for an academy meeting the end of that month. Later in the year, she'd attend the 1995 International Astronautical Congress in Oslo, Norway. The year after that, the congress would meet in Beijing.

Heath planned to continue her work with the Astronautical Academy. "I don't see a cut-off as long as there's a contribution, and that's a measure of people who ask you what you think." Her only problem with aging, she said, lay in the perception of others, being categorized as old.

In 1965, Heath received the Barbour International Air Safety Award. These words accompanied it: "for manifold contributions to aviation safety involving the establishment of a safety information exchange program; ...establishing liaison to further international cooperation in air safety; providing leadership in focusing attention and developing consensus in special problem areas such as search and rescue, and basic flight instruction. Improvements in air safety resulting from her untiring efforts..."

Another forty years of air and space safety activities followed. In September 1995, she was honored at a Women in Aerospace ceremony in Washington, D.C. Her citation was for lifetime achievement in that field.

She wrote later: "If I were to characterize myself, being constructive would be fundamental. And from there, it would be a wish to learn about problems and try to find a way out..."

12

Evelyn Foote, Brigadier General (Ret), born 1930; B.A., LLD (honorary) Wake Forest; M.A. Shippensburg State University; commanding general Fort Belvoir, Va.; commander 42nd Military Police, Germany; information officer U.S. Army hdgtrs., Vietnam; Bronze Star, Legion of Merit, Distinguished Service Medal; entered Women's Army Corps 1960, retired U.S. Army 1989.

B rig. Gen. Evelyn "Pat" Foote (Ret.) lived 20 to 25 miles southeast of Washington, D.C. Her house, like others in the new development, was tall, white-trimmed, traditional Southern, and appeared unconnected to the dreary little main street in Accokeek, Maryland, the community that provided her mailing address.

It's impossible to avoid a preconception of what a general looks like. And, of course, Gen. Foote didn't look like a general of the imagination. Medium tall, about 5-foot, 7-inches, and reed-slim, she wore a dark, flower print skirt and a black sweater under a white blazer. The small bar pinned in the lapel, she said, in answer to my question, was the Distinguished Service Medal.

Foote spoke softly, her word endings disappearing in a Southern upbringing.

Foote lived in Durham, North Carolina, through junior high then moved to Washington, D.C., where her parents worked for the federal government during the final years of World War II. After a couple of breaks before and during four years of college, Foote graduated summa cum laude from Wake Forest University in 1953. At that time, Foote recalled, "My baccalaureate in sociology would get me a good job as a caseworker or a secretary. I'd graduated into a work world that saw me in support roles, not a leader, never in charge of anything. No one gave a dang if I'd gone to college, they wanted to know if I knew how to type."

Her first job took her back to the FBI, where she'd worked earlier to earn tuition money. "The men," she said, "were in charge of it all in the FBI. Women couldn't be agents. I could have been the supervisor of the typing pool, but I didn't want that. A year later and after some thought, I left and became a copy girl with the old Washington Daily News—a Scripps-Howard paper.

"The only way you got to be a reporter then was to either come in with an established reputation or start at the bottom and see how many by-lined articles you could write while pushing copy. Well, I worked like crazy—10 hours a day, then out looking for a story. You had to find your own. At the end of a year I had some 20 by-lines and asked to be considered for a cityside assignment. They offered me writing on foods and fashions. The heck with that.

"I was recruited by Gray Line Sightseeing in Washington," she continued, "and had a brief stint as head of public relations, but after about a year, I found out I wasn't a huckster. I wrote because there was something worth writing about.

"So I left there for the security of Blue Cross and Blue Shield. They promoted me pretty quickly to what they called the enrollment secretary. That meant I could run the sales department, but I couldn't be a salesperson because I wasn't a man."

She was considering a job with the United States Information Agency when she met a woman Army officer. During college, Foote, like all students, received a pitch from the armed services. She'd tossed it out, unread.

"But seven years later," she said, "after talking with the first woman officer I'd ever met, and pursuing it more earnestly by phone, I realized I could be commissioned as a first lieutenant because of my age, degree and supervisory experience, and my pay—no matter how miserable—would be identical to a male's. Plus there would be opportunities for leadership experience. It sounded good.

"I had the advantage of being older and wiser. And most of us who came into the WAC (Women's Army Corps, organized 1942) in those years, came in at an older age. Many had been teachers and professors, in business, or self-employed.

"But this opportunity to work within the system, with pay equity, and to retire in 20 years if you elected to stay, was important. I said, 'What can I lose for two years?' So I did it for two years and, by the time I hung it up, I'd served for 29 years and seven months."

Her career lasted, Foote said, because of the old game of "stick and carrot." Every time she decided she'd had enough, she'd be offered something irresistible. At the 18 1/2 year point, the Army advised her to expect mandatory retirement at 20 years of service. She then commanded a battalion at Fort McClellan, Alabama. Because she'd been 29 when commissioned and 27 had been the top age for eligibility as a Regular Army officer, she'd served as a Reserve officer all of that time. But at the end of her command, she was offered promotion to colonel in the Regular Army. That automatically extended her tour of active duty for two years.

And when that promotion came through, she'd been named to the faculty of the Army War College. Rumors were she'd been considered for chief of staff at West Point which would have been another Army first. She'd told them, "You guys fight it out. I'll go wherever you want me to."

Her early career goals? "Because I was outrageously outspoken," Foote replied, "I hoped I might survive to retirement as a major—if I worked at it hard enough."

When she'd entered the Army, the highest rank a woman could rise to, permanent rank, was lieutenant colonel.

Only one woman held the rank of colonel and that was a temporary promotion. When replaced, the individual reverted to lieutenant colonel and the next woman up took the rank. At that time, there were only nine lieutenant colonels in the entire Women's Army Corps, other than in the medical sector, which Foote called a totally different career track.

"I guess once I had committed myself to the Army as a career," she said, "it was goals like—I'd love to serve in Europe. As it was, my first overseas assignment was Vietnam. Then, I'd love to make the rank of major and, if I ever am able, to go to the Command and General Staff College—or get my master's degree. So my goals changed as the times changed. We would go through periods when something was absolutely impossible, but then the next thing, you're picked to do it."

Proving herself came with every promotion. "I never had a job in the Army, above the rank of major, where I didn't have to," Foote said. "What happens is, when the men hear there's a woman coming, breaking up the old boy network, there's immediate suspicion that the reason she's there is because she's a woman, chosen to fill the quota.

"At the Army's Command and General Staff College, another student absolutely resented my presence because, in his mind, I'd prevented a male officer from getting requisite training. I said, 'What do you think this is to me?' I confronted him: 'You don't like my being here at all.' This caught him completely unexpectedly.

"I said, 'Maybe we can explore this a little so we'll understand why you resent me and maybe you can understand my position, too.' And we became friends. When I was on the faculty of the War College, I called him back to lecture on installation command and management. He'd ended up as a post commander, a very tough job, and he was able to tell students the kind of skills that you had to bring to that job.

"You just had to go in recognizing that, often, people would resent your being there. Just accept that as a given and win them over—slowly and surely.

"Some women simply couldn't stand it. They said, 'Hey, I will not put up with it.' But it's not putting up with it; like it or not, it's your role to continue educating the ignorant because in the future, we're going to need women more and more in these jobs."

Foote wrote in *Military Leadership* (Sage Publications, 1981), that she'd hoped for a post in San Francisco or Hawaii as her first military assignment. Instead she found herself in the dust and heat of rural Alabama, in charge of training successive platoons of 38, 18-to 34-year-old, women recruits. She also wrote that the experience made her want to be an Army officer forever, not just for the two years she'd planned on.

"I found out then how much I liked working with young people," she explained. "How much I enjoyed getting them at an impressionable point in their lives and trying to get them headed in a direction that would benefit their future.

"I wasn't planning to make them career soldiers—that's an individual choice—but to make them understand self-discipline as an absolutely essential part of creativity. 'We're all over you to help you get the kind of job you want; to make you more efficient in time-management.' Sometimes it took seven weeks. For others it wasn't until the last day that the light bulb went on."

Many years later, she continues to hear from some of her first recruits. They write her how well their lives turned out. They may not give her credit, but they remember her, want to share their successes.

"I found I really loved working with troops and was fortunate to have command to the extent I did," she said. "Typically, a woman might get a couple of commands. In the 1960s, we had only one battalion in the entire Army that a woman could lead. We had to change regulations by the dozen in order to command men—we could command women, not men. I could not even go to the Army War College until we got policies changed.

"Change became built into the military at about that time and we had to be able to accommodate change at a rate that was blinding and continues now. Just consider what's happened in the last three or four years: Women in the Navy can now serve on any classification of ship except submarines, at least until submarine berthing areas are modified. Women can fly combat aviation.

"It took a change in the law for this to happen and there are still many groups who are active opponents, including men who continue to send, through back channels, unsigned letters to commanders, columnists, and correspondents saying women aren't competent in these areas."

Key legislation in 1967 removed barriers to female, regular Army, enlisted strength and to ceilings on grade structure for women officers. But the most sweeping change came with the advent of the All-Volunteer Force in the early 1970s, when the draft ended. The time was right: the women's movement, civil rights, a human goals movement in the Department of Defense.

"In the early '70s," Foote said, "there had been general panic on the part of senior defense staff. Where were we going to get volunteers to serve in the numbers needed? Part of that answer was qualified women. So all of this came together and I was in the right place at the right time."

Foote served on the WAC director's staff in the Pentagon during the first part of the 1970s, when the plan for the greatly increased use of women soldiers was just getting underway—and, she said, "giving the Army-at-large a massive case of indigestion." She advised high-level commanders concerning the integration of women into previously male units.

On October 1, 1978, the office of the Director of the Women's Army Corps—then Major General Mary E. Clarke—was dissolved.

"The handwriting was on the wall," Foote said, "and she had absolutely no choice in the disestablishment of the WAC. While all of us had a truly great love and regard for the Women's Army Corps—what it was and what it did—it was time for the Corps to go. The only way women would receive a greater acceptance in the Army main stream was to get rid of the female bias. Then women's training would be similar to men's. We'd all be on the same sheet of music.

"I just read recently that according to some survey, the military is the institution Americans trust most. What a flip flop. The all-volunteer Army, which started out in such a poor posture to be an effective force, has evolved, over time and with some darned good leadership, to be the finest military force we've ever had, with the most intelligent, educated men and women serving on active duty of their own volition.

"But along the way, things happened that constantly had the public reeling—like deploying mothers to the Persian Gulf. But the point is, if we are going to have a volunteer force, then that force must be permitted to have a life as close to real life as anybody else. Like you can be yanked up and jerked halfway across the world tomorrow and you hope someone is going to be taking care of your kids. If this is what you choose to do—be a professional as well as married and have children—then it is your responsibility to ensure child care plans are in place at all times.

"There were a lot of do-gooders who wanted to bring all the mothers back from the Gulf and the mothers would have screamed their heads off. These were their careers."

Foote never married, though she recalled a "couple of close encounters." Up until the 1970s, she said, women who married and became pregnant had no choice but to leave the service. At that time, her career was foremost.

"The other thing," she said, "is that in the fifties, I was entirely too uppity for most men. I mean, 'What is this garbage—picking up your clothes, cleaning up after you? We both work. You do your share, too.' A lot of guys don't like that. And I wasn't going to just go home and sit—with or without children. So I wasn't the best candidate.

"There was such a movement after World War II, as women my age all know, to get us back into the home and the men back on the job. That pertained to the armed services, too. Rules and regulations on women's service were so stringent that women who were serious about their career, hesitated to give it up for the sake of saying you're married."

She grinned. "I just get more pickety and more persnickety and the longer I'm like this—one of these independent, unmarried women—the more it's going to take on the part of someone to convince me to give it up."

As far as parenthood, Foote believed any woman who hadn't become a mother undoubtedly wondered if she would be better at it than those she saw around her and that, she said, is a question that can't be answered. But Foote believed she hadn't really missed out on parenthood since she worked with young men and women throughout her entire career.

"I used to declare, I may not be married, but I'm in labor all the time with these kids. And that was true from the time I commanded a company until my final tour as commander of a post."

To be successful in a command position required highly developed leadership skills and Foote explained her leadership abilities in relation to how she, as battalion commander, worked with five commanders under her who trained the 800 to 1,000 troops continuously flowing through the system.

"First, I let them call the shots," Foote said. "I underwrote their failures and their trial-and-error learning. Second, I was available whenever they wanted to see me. Third, I took on the dragons in the training base and at higher headquarters who failed to give us the support we needed. That included everything from getting clothing and boots for the soldiers to getting good people to school on schedule and into decent assignments. Fourth, I backed my commanders.

"I believe (leadership) may be a matter of caring for all of your soldiers, caring enough to demand a lot from them in the way of performance and high standards. And they don't want things to be easy. Tough and fair, that's the program they're after."

Her experience with today's young volunteers, Foote said, told her they were not a great deal different than those she knew

20 years ago. And, she added, "I've commanded men and women and while there are bona fide differences between the sexes which must be dealt with, standards of performance and soldierly behavior are not negotiable."

The phone rang and Foote left to answer it. The house interior appeared as traditional as the exterior: wing-backed chairs next to the raised fireplace in the family room; couch against the wall. In the eating area where we sat, shelves held cookbooks, glass, and pottery. A magazine for runners lay on the counter in the kitchen. The wall by the table was glass and looked out from a second floor level at young trees, some with birdhouses, all leafless on that end-of-March day. Beyond stretched new homes with grass and landscaping yet to come.

Foote said earlier she'd looked at houses in other areas adjacent to Washington, D.C., but couldn't afford them. Development in the area where she was had just started, and she'd been able to get in by pooling funds with a friend, also a retired Army officer, sharing the house.

When Foote returned, I asked about her early life. "We—I had two brothers—were Depression kids in North Carolina," she said. "I was the youngest. Both of my parents worked so my brothers reluctantly brought—dragged—me up. You grow up in a special way when you're fighting for your life with two older brothers.

"From the time you're about five-years-old, you'd better be punching it out with the best of them. We'd fight like cats and dogs, but my parents would never know unless something was broken, a tooth missing, or a patch of skin discolored. No wonder I'm so aggressive. It was a survival skill. But what a wonderful way to learn rough and tumble—in a contained situation.

"There were no little girls in our neighborhood, all little boys. I played boys' softball, boys' football. I was very happy playing football until one day my mother watched out the window and realized I was the only person being tackled in touch football. That was my last day on the team."

Had her parents approved of her choice of career? "I think my parents loved my career though, initially, they didn't want me to do it," she replied. "Not for the reasons I thought—that women who go into the military are cheap, or something's wrong with them, or they have a screw loose—just because they would like to have had me home. But I think they were extremely proud of my career and took pleasure in it."

She recalled that in Vietnam she wrote them after the death of a reporter with whom she'd had dinner the night before. He'd been shot traveling with troops on a search and destroy mission. That kind of news, she realized, wasn't what parents wanted to hear and she didn't make the same mistake again.

Had there been individuals in her early life who had influenced her future? She remembered two: one, an uncle who had attended Wake Forest University in North Carolina and talked her into going there instead of George Washington, the university closest to the family home; the second, the Wake Forest dean of women.

"She was a tremendous woman," Foote said, "and a wonderful role model. For one thing, she gave me permission to work which was a no-no for freshmen. But I convinced her that if I didn't work, I couldn't stay in school." Foote admitted that, while working plus classes had been difficult, it had an up side too: "It sort of focuses you in a hurry on what you're there for."

In 1949, at the end of her freshman year, funds gone, she decided it would make more sense to go back to Washington, D.C., live at home, find a job, and continue college studies at George Washington University. She stayed a year, but missed Wake Forest and returned. Again the dean allowed her to work and also directed her toward a number of scholarships. Before the final semester of her senior year, Foote borrowed money to finish the term. "I wanted to find out what it was like to be just a student for one semester," she said. "I had a real good time."

After considering whether she'd made any major mistakes in her life, she said, "For a long time, I used to wonder, in my mind,

Evelyn Foote

if I had made a mistake in my professional development because I was always such a nut on medicine.

"But it took me six years to get my baccalaureate. The thought of trying to go beyond that to med school, without a dime to my name—I guess I didn't want it bad enough. Ultimately, I resolved it that way: If I'd wanted it bad enough, I'd have found a way.

"Not marrying: Was that a mistake? It doesn't seem to have kept me from having a very full life and working with young people. Perhaps giving up time I could have spent with my family was a mistake. And my mom and dad are both deceased now."

Foote said what made her efforts worthwhile was the realization that she could have a profound impact on many young men and women—on the quality of their lives, their education, their experience.

"And I think it was this," she continued: "A profound belief in the power of one to change things. One person, if prepared to stand up and be counted and take the guff, can make a difference. It takes a thick skin to convince an institution that is so conservative by its very nature that it's really behind the times most of the time, so advanced in some ways, so very backwards in others, that people who have earned a reputation for credibility and competence and logic, can point the way to a better position if they're willing to do it."

Foote grinned: "Every day was an adventure. Like who am I going to offend today? How can I offend thee? Let me count the ways.

"If it wasn't Phyllis Schlafley, it could be the Chief of Staff of the Army because I told him he screwed up. They don't like being told that. It was exciting and no matter how many arguments we had, how many fights, nose to nose, the Army always gave me a better job. 'Let's put her over here. Maybe we won't hear from her for awhile...'"

Job pressures went with every level of her career and she developed interests totally outside the military to balance that.

"I've always loved music—choral music, choirs, singing—and have been involved in music during my entire career, one place or another," she said. "I play a ukelele and now a Kimball organ. I'm a voracious reader. I like history, but when I'm on 'illiterature,' I love mysteries, to try to solve them. I like concerts and plays and travel. My housemate—she's out shopping now—and I hitchhiked with the Air Force out of Dover Air Force Base to England. Heard they had a plane going that day. Got on. The flight over and back cost us each $4.80—a meal going and a meal coming back. When the Air Force hauls cargo and has room for passengers, and you've signed up and are there, you can go. Now we're planning in the fall to hitchhike to bases in the Azores and to Italy and rent a car and go to Slovenia. The month before England, I toured both coasts of Florida because I'd never seen it all before.

"Next month I'm off to Italy and North Africa with the American Battle Monuments Commission. We're appointed by the President and we have the responsibility for operation and maintenance of every American military cemetery and many memorials overseas. Last year we were in Normandy for D-Day and two of us are going to Italy for this inspection trip. Three of us are working on another World War II memorial to be built in the Washington area. I thought I was getting out of memorials when I finished with the women's, but I found out that was just a warm-up."

Foote is a consultant as well. "From time to time, I go into the Pentagon on Army issues, or to schools as a speaker on defense personnel issues. What do I think the outcome will be on initiatives to increase opportunities for women in the military? Will women ever serve in combatant roles?"

In spite of changes, double standards still exist, she noted. "We have a dichotomy. The Army at the top is led by men whose principal experience has been combat and leading men. They have very little experience in leading women. But suddenly these four-stars are at the helm of the Army as the least exposed exponents of an integrated force, and they are not about to rock the ship and put women into ground combat. Now I'm not advocating taking off all the restrictions, but if we ever want to get the answers as to whether or not women would be effective as soldiers in the combat army—well, you never know until you try.

"If we were ever to mobilize again, and given the experience of other armies and other nations, combat for women seems a possibility. The use of women in combat was common in Russia, for example, and in Israel's early years. Today Israel trains women in arms, but does not use them in combat roles. But they're trained should there be a need for them in a defense situation."

When speaking at service schools and private organizations, she relates personal memories of what she and other women went through—their trials and tribulations in opening opportunities for women in the 1960s, '70s and '80s.

She advises women that if they do not continue to fight for their rights to serve in the positions where they feel they can make the best contribution, those rights will be lost.

"I could just sit and enjoy my retirement and do nothing but play, but it seems to me that in every generation of women, those with leadership roles have a responsibility to move the institution, to move the flag, forward a hundred yards.

"I'm sorry to say at this point, for whatever reason, there are few women serving on active duty willing to stand up and be counted. I think part of it is a natural fear at a time of tremendous downsizing. What would be their future if they spoke out against the system? Well, I was raised in the Women's Army Corps, and we were nothing but a bunch of adventurers anyway.

"The only way we survived in this tremendous man's world in the '50s and '60s and after World War II when they were trying to step on us one more time—to our mortal disadvantage—was by standing up, piping up and fighting back. And that's how I was raised. You can be a doormat, or you can stand up and let them know you don't like what they're planning to do."

Foote continued to rattle cages. She'd recently testified, in Federal District Court in Brooklyn, against the ban on gays and lesbians in the military. "I expect my Pentagon pass to be pulled immediately," she said with a grin, "but I said nothing then that I hadn't said before.

"I sincerely feel—again flying in the face of the majority—that we are totally hypocritical when we recognize and acknowledge the presence in the service of women—and men—whose orientation may not be heterosexual, but at the same time, muffle them from ever being revealed for that orientation. And, in fact, if revealed will see to their discharge. To me, it is truly unconstitutional to discriminate for nothing more than orientation, immediately assuming misconduct will follow.

"Most women in the military have their own horror stories of harassment by heterosexual males and, in fact, the far greater offense in the military, largely unheeded, is the continued harassment of women by men. Speak out and you're liable to be targeted for investigation. You're liable to be sent to the psychiatrist.

"This policy has very effectively been used against women. We've had men proposition a woman and when they're turned down, immediately spread rumors that she's queer. Many women have left the service rather than put up with it. This particular policy is being used as a club and a hammer.

"Many serving officers will tell you very positively, this is a tempest in a teapot. We've had lesbians and homosexuals in our forces forever, and they're among our best troops. As long as they don't bring misconduct to the workplace—and that goes for adulterers too. As long as the rules are in place."

Six claimants, five men and one woman, had taken the Defense Department to court on the grounds that the "don't ask, don't tell," policy was unconstitutional. Foote believed that even if the judge ruled in favor of the military, the appeal would continue until it reached the Supreme Court.[1]

"I've done stressful things in my life," she said, "but I can't think of a thing I've done recently that was more stressful than openly opposing, by testifying, a policy of the organization in which I serve. But I felt in this instance, where the system is not self-correcting, then it must go to the courts. That's how we changed many discrepancies in the laws and policies impacting women. And in that way, the service doesn't bear the onus of having made a decision that will be unpopular in some circles."

A typical day begins early and actively for Foote. She jogs, walks, uses a Nordic track and rowing machine.

"I've been blessed with good health all my life, and I've got more energy than I sometimes know what to do with," she said. "As far as growing older, people's perception of aging bothers me, but aging doesn't bother me.

"I think eventually, when I no longer feel a desire or need to stay as involved as I am in projects and organizations, I'll probably leave this area. I love Washington, but it's prohibitively expensive and the traffic is incredible. I figure it would be nice to be where you could look at mountains and water and not give up so many of your resources just maintaining a house and property. I also think as I grow older, I'll want to scale down on the size of my house—my lord, four bedrooms, full basement—cut down to what I want to take care of. To be freer. To travel. To see friends and family. I believe that no matter how actively you are involved, as you are removed further and further in time from active service in the military, what you can contribute becomes less and less.

"The military gave me a wonderful career and I'll always be interested in the military and its welfare, but it will not be my driving concern forever."

We went back down the long entry hall to her office and library for a photograph. Major attractions of the small room included a cello in one corner; a wall of books; and a foot-high teddy bear wearing camouflage gear, combat boots, and a cap with a star.

Foote picked up the bear: "I'm trying to cut back on my possessions, but I can't bring myself to part with this." She put the bear back in the chair. "There are many people who think you got your star because you never made waves," she said. "You make waves through your whole career. But you make waves within the system and try to work within the system to achieve more equity. You don't go to the newspapers or the talk shows. You alter things within the system, in the system, and that's the way I worked."

Fraser packed up his cameras and I made a restroom stop before the trip back to Washington. In the guest bathroom, there was a framed piece on the wall. Just words: "Some leaders are born women."

1. A week after the interview, at the end of March, 1995, Judge Eugene Nickerson ruled the policy violated the First and Fifth Amendment rights of gay troops to appease the bigotry of heterosexual soldiers. Though the ruling applied only to the six active-duty and reserve service members who filed the lawsuit, newspaper reports on the decision said the ruling set a precedent and would likely encourage others to challenge the policy known as "don't ask, don't tell, don't pursue." Nickerson dismissed the government's argument that without the ban, morale, discipline, and even privacy for heterosexuals would dissolve. The Justice Department indicated it would appeal.

13

Ah Quon McElrath, born 1915 in Honolulu;
began fighting the wrongs of the world in college and hasn't stopped: hired by the
longshoremen's union as its first social worker,
her programs became models: she's been re-
discovered by women's studies and featured
in a TV documentary.

A h Quon McElrath met me at the Columbia Inn in downtown Honolulu. The clientele looked local. The decor was
sports. Framed National Football League jerseys, posters,
and sports art hung on the walls. In what once had been a baked
goods display case, a football signed by Dick Butkus perched next
to a photo of him on the field. Nearby sat a Riddell Jets helmet
and, in a plastic box, a baseball signed by Hank Aaron. Booths
ran parallel to the counter and in rows behind it. We drank iced tea
in the booth farthest back and adjusted voice volume to other con-
versations and the clink of dishes on plastic tables.

A friend, a Honolulu journalist, described McElrath as elo-
quent and brilliant. I saw a small woman, slight, 4-foot, 10- or 11-
inches; olive skin; short, tousled dark hair streaked with gray. There
was a coiled-spring air to her; seated, she looked in motion.

Ah Quon, born to Chinese immigrants, arrived next to the
last of seven children.

I Can't Do What?

"My father died when I was four-and-a-half," she said. "I was a working class kid, born poor, lived with the poor. No one had any more than anyone else, except maybe the guy who drove a taxi. At least he had his car."

Also part of the experience was changing community rules. "There was a period when they said, 'Let the Chinese smoke opium; it's part of their culture.' Then official attitudes shifted. That's when my father went to prison. Not unusual in the neighborhood. So what the hell? It's no big deal. But what happens is the only picture of my father was painted from a snapshot stolen from prison records by my sister."

A deprived childhood? No way. In intermediate school, inspired by creative teachers, Ah Quon dove into whatever came along—news writing, literature, economics, and classical music.

"My brother and I shared chores in the kitchen—where the radio was—on Saturday afternoons," she said. "We'd sing along with the Texaco opera broadcasts. We knew all the arias."

Earlier when in intermediate school, on her own, she'd dropped after-school Chinese language courses to concentrate on English, since, she said, "there was no indication I would live anywhere but in the U.S." In high school the debate coach recruited her and she traveled with the team to San Francisco to defeat two high schools in decision debates.

"What the debate thing did was reinforce my feeling that the written and spoken word, done well, became a very powerful instrument. The realization was that I would learn to read, write, and speak English in the best way I could."

Her interest in the labor movement, captured by books she read in high school, coincided with a good deal of activity at the local level. In 1935, the year after she graduated, the Wagner Act, or National Labor Relations Act, now called the most important single piece of labor management legislation, passed the U.S. Congress.

Meanwhile, Ah Quon, a child of the Depression, never imagined getting to college except through her own efforts. She hustled up five jobs and worked her way to a bachelor's degree in sociology, with honors in anthropology, from the University of Hawaii in 1938.

During these years, her future took on a shape. "At that time," she recalled, "the seamen and longshoremen began organizing. In 1938, during a longshoremen's and seamen's strike, I'd go to the park and listen to speeches. I volunteered to put up posters... The CIO put out the 'Voice of Labor' newspaper and I'd buy that from the Dew Drop Inn, along with the New Masses magazine, both of which presented the world from a different point of view."

By then she'd already participated in campus peace marches against German militarism and the Spanish Civil War and helped organize meetings on these and other controversial issues.

After college, she volunteered in the territory's welfare bureau which administered aid to children and families and individuals as part of the Social Security Act.

Other key events occurred. In 1938, she met Robert McElrath, a seaman, active in the union movement on the West Coast of the United States and member of the Marine Firemen, Oilers and Wipers Association; then met him again in 1940 when, at the request of union organizer Jack Hall, he arrived to support strikers on the island of Kauai. Ah Quon identified that strike as a landmark since common grievances united Filipinos and Japanese for the first time. Previously, the various ethnic groups, who worked and lived separately on the islands' plantations, had seldom cooperated on labor issues.

She married Bob McElrath in 1941. Again, Ah Quon's personal history shifted into ideology. McElrath worked then as a machinist with Inter-Island Steamship and Navigation Company.

"Nothing much was happening on the waterfront at that time," she said. "The longshoremen's union wasn't terribly effective so Bob organized the first independent union at Inter-Island, which had figured so prominently in the 1938 longshoremen's and seamen's strike."

How effective were their early union efforts to change working conditions? "We never did get closed shops," McElrath said, "but we did get automatic deductions for union dues and charities. During the war years, besides Inter-Island, we also organized Hawaiian Tuna Packers, American Can, and Hawaiian Pineapple Company."

In 1954, the International Longshoremen's and Warehousemen's Union leadership hired her as its first social worker. "At that time," she said, "the union had begun negotiating for members' fringe benefits—medical plans, pension plans—things that affected members' lives outside of their jobs, and that would be the kind of work I would be involved with."

Harry Bridges, legendary leader of the longshoremen, and her husband were members of the all-male committee that hired her. Her husband cast the only negative vote—on the grounds of nepotism. He was overruled.

"They wanted someone who knew social work and was honest, and they knew I was these things because they'd worked with me when I'd volunteered during earlier strikes," McElrath recalled. "I'd done investigation of need among union members after the April 1, 1946, tidal wave which did major damage on the island of Hawaii. Later in 1946, there'd been a strike—which had begun Labor Day—by sugar workers against 26 sugar plantations and involving more than 28,000 workers, not including family members. I'd also volunteered as a social worker then, doing educational work—getting recipes for nutritious meals from the Department of Health, helping start a free school lunch program, working with creditors, banks, and utilities, that sort of thing."

Two men stopped by the table. McElrath introduced them. They'd worked together on a community committee. Animated, her hands moved constantly. She talked rapidly, asked questions, finished sentences, filled in gaps.

When the men left, she continued: "In 1949, during a strike by 5,000 longshoremen, I really did some heavy extensions of this kind of thing—again as a volunteer. I got tuition waived for their

Ah Quon McElrath

kids going to the private (religious) schools, helped set up soup
kitchens where strikers and their families could be fed: did some
real hard training sessions. And probably, most importantly, I got
people together, and this was important to sustain morale."

Looking back at milestones in her career, she recalled efforts
to get a handle on excessive health care costs which had led to a
threat by insurers to cut coverage of workers at the port of Hilo.
She researched claims, looking at cultural and environmental fac-
tors. After meeting and talking with families, she worked out a
program addressing nutrition, sanitation, and behavior patterns and
introduced family planning. She helped to set up a health maintenance, nurse-run system with the Kaiser Foundation health plan
for spouses and retired workers of Oahu Sugar Company.

"I was the only social worker, but I expanded my influence
by training secondary leadership," McElrath said. "We did inno-
vative stuff—like 'These are the helping agencies,' 'This is how
the police work;' how to detect alcohol abuse, what resources are
available for solutions to problems bosses saw on and off the job.

I ran education sessions on workplace accidents and absenteeism so secondary leaders could chart problems and then follow the numbers."

There's no question in McElrath's mind about the effectiveness of what she could do with the union as opposed to what she'd done as a public employee.

"As a social worker for the union," she said, "I had a lot more possibilities for creativity, for expanding on that which is still the basic reason for what it is that makes a union click. The trade union is one of the only avenues to give individuals some measure of control over their working lives. The kind of social work I did extends this measure of control, and if you happen to believe like I do, that this is what it's all about in a democratic society, you have to do that kind of work.

"The other kind means I am a party to an onslaught on a person's civil liberties. Take a look at all the social legislation that's been enacted affecting the poor and there's just no doubt that those who receive public assistance live the most controlled and regulated lives of anybody in the United States. If you believe in democracy, you simply cannot go for that."

If she had a role model, it was social worker Bertha Reynolds, a Smith College graduate. Like Reynolds, who'd worked with the National Maritime Union on the East Coast, McElrath never hid her political beliefs.

No, she said, she is not a communist, "I'm a left winger and that ideological bent was always there. That to me has been a way of analyzing the way of the world. I don't believe you're worth anything if you waffle."

She considered the skills involved in her work: "being able to help union members navigate their way through huge bureaucracies; respect for the individual's abilities, dignity; being able to convey basic information. That's not what you learn in college. Education in social work is training in things like conducting interviews. But you can alter academic learning to become a true educator of other people."

As to the sacrifices her career required, she said, "I don't know if you'd call it that, but during the strikes you had to live through a great deal of venom—people hissing, 'goddamn communists, always closing ports.' At one time I ran for a PTA office—PTA—and there was a vast protest—letters to the paper—how could we have a communist PTA officer? It was my children, called 'commie rats' by their classmates, who suffered more. It was the hurt to the human heart and mind that was great, especially to kids growing up."

During this period, her husband appeared before the House Un-American Activities Commission, one of the Reluctant 39 who took the Fifth Amendment. She was called but the subpoena was quashed. "They probably figured one McElrath was enough," she said.

"The payoff was being able to make the lives of working people a great deal more comfortable than their forebears who came to Hawaii early in the game. Our political efforts gave them a better sense of their rights, made it possible for them to vote in a more cogent fashion. Gave them opportunities to run for office themselves, to help make decisions on social policies. I believe we gave them a sense of dignity they'd never had before, through control of their work by collective bargaining, through involvement in the political processes. Maybe a more indefinable thing—what their role in society truly is."

McElrath retired from the union staff in December 1981. "I horsed around for awhile," she said, "then 1983 to 1985 worked for the Villiers Foundation in Washington, D.C. At the time, this foundation, established by a Frenchman who wanted to give something back to the United States, was devoting its efforts to the problems of senior citizens. When I was there, we accomplished the first major changes to the Supplemental Security Income program since 1974 when Aid to the Aged and Blind and Aid to the Disabled had been absorbed."

Back home, McElrath was asked to help organize a committee on welfare concerns. These efforts produced an increase of 10 percent in public assistance from the Hawaiian legislature in 1987—the first increase in nine years. In 1988, the method of payment, through the efforts of the committee, changed to a percentage of the federal poverty level, initially at 60 percent then increased to 62.5 percent, thus ensuring an annual cost of living allowance for welfare recipients.

"These," she said, "are the political battles one has to fight on behalf of poor people. No one ever worries about the poor."

McElrath shook her head: "The whole political process is fascinating—when you can begin to make changes. When you cannot. Do you get your foot in the tent or ask for the whole bundle?"

Though she and her husband had lived apart for the previous 10 years, she said, they remained friends. For the past two years he'd been ill and a short time before the interview, she'd made different living arrangements for him. She's on call when he needs help.

These days, McElrath lobbies on issues such as welfare and health care during legislative sessions, talks to university classes, and participates in seminars and various community groups. She'd been recorded by women's studies professors for oral histories and CNN included her in a documentary, "A Century of Women in America."

"There's just not enough people willing to take a stand," she said. "If you have a job and your perception is that the job depends on keeping quiet, you won't speak up (for what you believe). I do. No one can take away my Social Security or pension. I can be honest—say anything I damn well please."

14

Jean Lee Payne, correctional officer, counselor; born 1929; degrees Mills College, zoology, University of California, Berkeley, criminology; first woman director of major California correctional facility.

Jean Payne talked with the builder over a set of blueprints spread across a table saw. They, and the saw, balanced on cross beams of a foundation cut into a steep bank above Lake Chelan, a 55-mile long, fjord-like lake in the center of Washington state. On a raw, early January morning, low clouds hung over the lake, hiding mountain tops and fuzzing the gray outlines of apple orchards spread across the foothills.

Payne at that time lived in a compact apartment built over what would be the garage for her new house. Eighteen months earlier, her husband had died of a heart attack. After a few months, she'd sold their large house further up lake and bought a nearby lot. She'd worked out the design for the house going up, chosen a builder, arranged for removal of the old cottage on the site, and for the last few weeks had been making the dozens of daily decisions that home building required. Payne wore a purple duffle coat over jeans, appropriate to her life at that point. Down coats certainly weren't standard garb for the San Francisco Bay area where she'd lived until retiring to Chelan in 1981.

Chelan, an Americanized-spelling of an Indian word meaning deep water, was both a lake and a town of about 1,500 at the end of it. Payne lived 17 miles from the town and four miles from the end of the south shore road. Most of the lake past Payne lay in National Forest land, accessible only by boat or seaplane.

When Payne and her husband lived in California, they often stopped overnight in Chelan on their way to canoe rivers in Alaska and the Yukon. After a brief and unsuccessful try at Southern California retirement living, they'd come to Chelan.

Her conversation with the builder over, she led the way up the steps to her temporary residence. She planned to rent it when she moved into the new house. Like a proper Washingtonian, Payne's coffee started with the stutter of grinding beans. We drank it at a table between the kitchen and living area, down a short hall from a bedroom and bath. The apartment was light, neat, and new with many windows overlooking the lake. A computer and monitor sat on a desk by the stairway. Shelves around the perimeters of the room held papers, books, photos, tapes, and the assorted other possessions humans require.

Payne, oldest of three girls in her family, was born and grew up in Tacoma, Washington. Her father was an attorney; her mother, formerly a teacher, took care of her family and volunteered for various community causes. Like the prototypical young woman of her class and generation, Payne went from high school to college, Mills; met her husband, a returned World War II veteran finishing his studies at the University of California, Berkeley, under the GI Bill; and married the month after her graduation at 20.

"I promptly had three children and became a housewife, community volunteer, and part-time bridge player, just like my mother and every other woman I knew," Payne said. "In 1961, when my youngest went off to first grade, a friend said, 'Good. Now you can play bridge mornings, too.' I panicked."

"'I'm not going to be one of those,' I told my husband that night. 'I'll get a job.'

"'Fine,' he said. 'As long as you keep up the house and you're not too tired at night for sex.'

"Diploma in hand, I started job hunting. The question I was asked most often was, 'Can you type?'"

Her first job was at an Oakland department store, 11 to 3, so she'd be home when the children arrived from school. In a few months, she'd been promoted to a level where she faced longer hours and baby-sitters.

"At that point," Payne said, "I decided to look at a career rather than just a job.

"I went to Mills' placement office for some help and they suggested I start taking civil service exams. The first one was for probation officer in Alameda County—I didn't even know what the title meant—and I passed. The only part I remember of the oral interview later concerned what I would do if my children refused to do what I asked. In my house children did what I wanted. I thought they were nuts to ask such nonsense and I said so. I guess my 32-year-old bravado sounded like what they were looking for and I was working in a home for delinquent girls before I knew what hit me."

Her duties included teaching residents to cook and clean, "Like I'd been doing but now I got paid for it." Most of the staff were new college graduates and more or less by default, she ended up in a supervisory position. The system required two years before promotion and at the end of that time, she double-jumped up the ladder.

"I'd started as a line worker," Payne said, "but after I'd been there about a year and a half, we had big problems. The director had overspent the budget and we ran out of money three months before the next appropriation. Staff would be paid but we had no replacement money for sick leave, extra food—nothing. The director either quit or was fired and her good friend, the assistant director, quit with her. So from working deputy, I was suddenly promoted to assistant director. There was no director appointed immediately, so I filled that spot, too.

"I really didn't know what I was walking into. Basically, we had no money. But how do you learn how to handle money? Right. By being a housewife and living on a budget. Whether it's $300 a month—my husband's first salary—or $30,000, the principle is the same." Payne laughed. "I remember we had a storeroom full of toilet paper, extra towels, and I traded with other institutions for what we needed. Then I worked my fanny off, covering vacant shifts and helping with counseling, because I thought that's what you were supposed to do."

She ran the hall for several months, until a male from one of the boys' facilities was promoted to director. "At the time, I was glad to have someone come in," she said. "But he turned out to be totally incompetent and, what was worse, literally afraid of women."

In an institution for girls with a mostly female staff, he was in trouble. Remembered Payne, "Those were the worst two years I ever spent."

After a miserable and frustrating second year, she asked permission of her boss to talk over some of the hall's difficulties with their superior, director of juvenile institutions in the county. Why would no one listen to their needs, improve working conditions, or do something about her bosses' attitude?

"Have patience," the director told her. "We're trying to fire him." The situation grew even worse.

"It played out like a bad marriage," Payne recalled. "He literally didn't speak to me for the three months until he left. I probably would have stayed on except his replacement, whom I liked and admired, seemed to have a long lease on the job, and that made it a dead end for me. At the time, I found nothing unusual in being qualified as a director and doing the job for years and being overlooked because there'd never been a woman director. I didn't fight it. I wasn't a problem causer and there was no support for that kind of thing anyway. Not at that time."

For a year, Payne supervised investigating deputies who dealt with juvenile crime. This was in the 1970s and she was on the doorstep of Haight Ashbury, a focus of the enormous social changes the country was undergoing.

"We then had a different kind of youngster coming into custody," Payne said. "They were middle class, educated, flower-children types, over-involved with drugs and the streets, but not tough and definitely not criminal. They ran away, cut school, were beyond the control of themselves and their parents—what we called status types. Status crimes being defined by law as pertaining only to things that wouldn't be a crime at 21 years of age but were at 16 or 18."

"I was in the forefront of a movement that effectively changed the juvenile code in handling status crimes as family problems and used counseling as an alternative to incarceration.

"A group of us wrote a program and presented it to judges and probation brass and eventually I was appointed to run it—a department called the Family Crisis Intervention Unit. I stayed five years, training and supervising staff, teaching at local colleges and working with some of the top family therapists in the area."

The unit eventually became a prototype for diversion programs in California and then in Washington.

In the meantime, her husband had switched careers, becoming a probation officer in nearby Contra Costa County. They both went back to UC Berkeley to earn masters' degrees in criminology.

In the early 1970s, probation and welfare departments merged. Payne, eligible for a major appointment, was offered a job.

"I turned it down," she said. "That was unheard of. I was told I was disloyal, wasn't a team player... My response was, they already had women directors in welfare and it was time someone decided we could work in corrections as well. Their response was I'd just ensured I'd never be promoted and that was fine with me. I truly liked my position in the Family Crisis Unit."

If that was a bluff, it worked. In early 1975, Payne was appointed Director of Juvenile Hall in Alameda County. She became chief administrator of two juvenile halls, one with 35 beds in downtown Oakland, one with 300 beds in San Leandro.

The facility included a high school and medical clinic. The staff of 155, mostly men, included many ex-Oakland Raiders and former professional athletes.

"These were exceptionally good jobs for minorities—women and any ethnic groups—since we were paid the same as white males," Payne said. "The hiring requirements were two years of college. Many of the staff had four. We attracted top people because of the pay, because we had the same privileges as the military or police—including early retirement. And along with the challenge, there was an element of danger that was attractive."

What kind of a reception did she get, as the first woman in the state to head a major correctional institution? "They knew who I was," Payne said. "I'd worked closely with staff at the hall when we started the diversion program, done some training with them, so I wasn't an unknown quantity. Though I believe they were all a little shell-shocked when I got the job."

Staffing hierarchy was director, assistant director, two supervising deputies, and four senior counselors who ran shifts. "I was blessed with a fantastic assistant director," she said. "Before I came, staff would corner him and whisper, 'Do you know who the new director is?' He'd say, with a perfectly straight face, 'No. But you'll like her just fine.' He was Korean, an ex-Marine, and very bright. He knew the ropes, was willing to share, loyal, had no problems with a woman boss. Absolutely perfect."

However, three of the four senior counselors and a supervisor chose to retire within her first three months. "It was a good old boy world with those guys, all white males," she recalled, "and while nothing specific was said, they chose to go. I convinced the department to let me bring in two women who were just as good as and as tough as any man. This was the first time that women had supervised boys."

Resulting staff reassignments moved the remaining senior counselor to a post as trainer of new seniors.

"He'd been a professional basketball player in the days when black males were heavily discriminated against," Payne said. "He

Jean Lee Payne

was a wonderful worker, with a fine, intuitive feel for handling difficult youngsters and strong-minded staff. But he was angry, defensive and not about to give an inch. For these reasons, he'd been passed over for promotion many times. I'd certainly had my run-ins with him.

"I remember when I'd been told I'd been selected to be the director of the hall. A judge, the chief probation officer, lots of brass, were around the table. I must have looked stunned. 'What's the matter,' someone said, 'don't you think you can handle it?' I shook my head. 'I can handle it,' I said. 'But I was thinking of working with Mr. C.' Everyone laughed. They knew him."

Payne recalled Mr. C's first evaluation. For his abilities as supervising counselor, she had high praise; for his temper, negatives.

He stormed out of her office. The next day he was back. He'd talked it over with his wife who said the evaluation was absolutely right. So what could he do to change? From then on they worked well together.

I asked if a staff of macho athletes found it difficult to work for a woman. Payne shook her head: "Competent black men had strong mothers and wives and they dealt better with women than white men did. That the good old boys had quit was a break in the long run."

Though Payne got into the correctional field on a fluke—that was the first civil service exam after a Mills job counselor suggested she take that route to find work—she believed the career suited her character.

"If someone dumps a load of problems on the table, I literally don't question having to come up with a plan," she explained. "I remember when the money ran out in the girls' residence, when the three supervisors walked out, I thought, 'Now what?' I don't remember panicking. You're a mother with a lot of kids, you pick up the marbles and get on with it."

An "enlightened" chief probation officer had recommended her promotion to director and supported her all along the way. "He gave me the hall and let me run it. I didn't have people second guessing me or trying to cut me off at the pass.

"After I'd been director for about three months, I remember coming home on a Sunday and the children meeting me: 'The hall has been trying to get you.'

"We'd had a major fire. The staff had panicked and done all the wrong things—taken the kids out of their rooms and locked them in an upstairs dining hall, delayed calling the police while they tried to put the fire out. Everything was in a mess when I got there. Finally, everything got done. During the investigations that followed, as facts emerged, it became clear the fire started in a mattress, by a cigarette a staff member had given a detainee. Staff carelessness was evident throughout.

"At a big meeting afterward, the chief probation officer, instead of telling me what to do, asked, 'What do you want to do?' I had that kind of support all along and it was invaluable."

Payne talked of other such times. She decided to remove the dining room partitions which kept young male inmates divided into small groups, cover the institutional beige walls with color and graphics. A new director of food services, a former chef in an officers' club, had already added more vegetables and salads and wanted to start a buffet line.

"Well," recalled Payne, "all the old-timers knew if the kids stood in line, they'd kill each other. But my boss said, 'Sure, go ahead.' That first night when we reopened the dining hall, everyone stayed late, waiting to see the riot they knew would happen. But the food fight didn't happen—and never did.

"When I first came, the staff worried about me. The routine procedure was to make rounds every morning, read shift logs, check things out. We had four boys' units, from A to D, with A being the least worrisome and D where the tough guys were. That first morning I spotted a couple of counselors following me. 'You can't go there by yourself,' they said. 'They'll jump you, hold you hostage.'

"I said, 'Look, I'm supposed to run this place. I don't need a bodyguard.' And I did that every morning for two and a half years and nothing happened."

Other job hazards included bomb threats—the institution received many—and unannounced visits by any public official or authority that had anything to do with juveniles, sometimes looking only for an excuse to attract media attention.

Problems and all, Payne loved her job. She stayed two-and-a-half-years.

"Our children were grown and gone by then. I probably would have kept on working," she said. "My job gave me lots of perks—recognition, good income, challenges, and satisfaction. But Fred had retired and by then, I'd had 20 years in the correction system and was eligible for retirement. Fred had a couple of bouts of cancer and one morning I just woke up and asked myself, 'Why am I working this hard when I don't have to?'"

They sold their home and bought a condominium in Coronado, a beach community in Southern California.

"Fred, facing his cancer, went into a major depression and I went through a lot of 'what are we going to do with our lives?'"

she said. "We played bridge and tennis, took classes at the University of California at San Diego, which has a fine seniors' program. But we still couldn't find a way to make our life have meaning. Then we started moving around in the camper and found Chelan.

"We ended up here in 1981 and both found out what we could do best. Fred got involved in fixing up our old house and garden. I set up a counseling practice. It flourished and I began to get involved in community life. Our oldest son, an actor by avocation, arrived and dragged his father on stage."

Payne put her managerial skills to work backstage. She became chairman of the board of Bach Feste, an annual week of musical events, produced musicals, and was elected to the hospital board. A year or two before the interview, she'd been named the Chamber of Commerce's Citizen of the Year.

Then Fred died and Payne had to adjust again, was still adjusting. "I would say at this time, I'm dealing with widowhood more than old age or anything else," she said. "Suddenly I feel cut off from a whole way of life. We had a great relationship, shared a sense of adventure, and had a lot of fun. I don't want to quit being in the world now that I'm no longer a couple, but I have to find out how."

She was dating again, but worried about what it would take to adjust to living with someone else after 43 years of another marriage. She did believe she was finding answers even though the thought of facing years alone wasn't a pleasant one.[1]

She took the cups to the sink and then followed her exuberant Chesapeake Bay retriever down the stairs and outside. We watched the builder work.

I asked why, on that long ago day, she'd chosen to look for work rather than join the morning bridge group?

"Because I was a misfit," she said. "PTA, charity meetings bored me. I'd sit and think, 'Is this all we're going to talk about—all we're going to do?' I truly thought there was something wrong with me that what I had wasn't enough.

"I joined a discussion group at the library and talked too much. Someone told me I did, that I was too intense. I thought, 'I cannot live this way. I want out.' My father raised hell when I went to work. He said, 'You'll lose your husband and your children will become juvenile delinquents.' My husband said, 'Whatever you want to do.' And he stood by that. I couldn't have done it otherwise.

"I could have stayed home. Not doing that was my choice. Today many women don't have a choice and I think that's too bad. We need those choices."

1 Late in 1995, Payne remarried. Her husband is also widowed. Madison Vick is a musician from Oregon and she's known him since he came to Chelan to play in the Bach Feste orchestra several years ago. They live in her new home at the lake.

15

Muriel Siebert, born 1933 in Cleveland, found financial fame in New York City; college dropout; nine honorary doctorates; visiting professor, Harvard, Dartmouth, New York University.

The appointment—hard to pin down from word one—was at 11 a.m. Muriel Siebert had not yet arrived. A modest waiting room came with a half-dozen straight-backed chairs, financial reading, and wall displays of relevant material. The latter included a page one, 1980 New York Times photo of Siebert, then New York's Superintendent of Banking, sprawled in a chair, exhausted after a long legislative session; a newspaper story headlined "First NY Exchange Seat for Woman Sought by Analyst;" New York Stock Exchange certification; a lifetime achievement award from New York Mayor David Dinkins; woman of the year award from a White House conference on small business; and a 3-by 4-foot painting of the floor of the New York Stock Exchange.

A receptionist fielded ringing phones, visitors and deliveries. In an adjacent room, people at rows of desks looked at blue computer screens. Eleanor, Siebert's secretary, whom I'd talked with often during past weeks, led the way through her office to Siebert's.

That morning's taping of a television program featuring her boss had started late, Eleanor said. Siebert was on her way.

We sat at a table in the corner, looking past a potted palm into Manhattan windows. Siebert's Third Avenue offices were on the 17th floor of the "Lipstick Building." That's what people in New York City called the rounded and gleaming maroon building with multi-storied, dusky rose pillars out front.

Siebert's office came with as much Siebert memorabilia as the reception area. Among these were photos of her with Presidents Reagan, Carter, Bush, and Nixon. A plaque, "The Banker," was draped with a wide, red-velvet ribbon anchored by a saucer-sized medallion, "National Women's Hall of Fame 1994."

The room was large and light with shelves running under a wall-to-wall bank of windows. An open door offered another look into the area of desks and computers. That room was very large and not partitioned. On the floor near Siebert's desk were a couple of dog dishes and a box of dry dog food in a milk-carton type of container. Several dog toys lay scattered about.

Fairly soon, Eleanor followed Siebert in. Siebert gave the tiny dog she carried to Eleanor who unsnapped its leash and peeled off its sweater. Siebert dropped things on her desk, glanced at what was on it, came to the table, and sank bonelessly into a chair.

A short woman with chin-length, straight, turned-under-at-the-ends blonde hair, she was dressed that morning in black slacks, silky blouse, and checked jacket.

She and Eleanor, one of her two black secretaries, talked briefly: why she was late—shooting time had changed, she hadn't gotten the message; the need to switch garages where she took her car for repair. Eleanor left, dog under her arm, and Siebert began the second interview of her day with a job description.

"I own Muriel Siebert and Company, Inc.," she said. "We're members of the New York Stock Exchange. We have 80,000 accounts. Part of the activities of my firm is discount brokerage. Part of the work we do is Siebert Capital Markets which is the institutional and underwriting arm of the firm. We underwrite new issue securities, and we go into underwritings which we place with institutions and other accounts.

"That is what I do for a living. I do a lot of pro bono for my soul.

"The talent I bring to it is, I guess, that I could do any of those functions as well as anyone else in the firm. I don't do it now because I own the place, and it's grown, and I spend a lot of time on future planning. But there was a time I could work orders on the floor of the New York Stock Exchange as good as my institutional equity desk because that's what I did for a living. I know how to take orders and I know how to work the orders on the floor. I know what post to go to. I know how to handle orders. And I can analyze underwritings we get involved in because I started out as a research trainee."

What made much of this possible was membership in the New York Stock Exchange, something that no woman held until Muriel Siebert came along. She'd covered a lot of ground and acquired many firsts since then, but that's what she's known for on Wall Street.

"I made the stock exchange co-ed," was how Siebert put it. "I'd asked one of my customers where I could go to get credit on the accounts. He was male: They didn't have partners in major firms that were women.

"He said, 'I don't think you can. Why don't you buy a seat and work for yourself?'

"I said, 'Don't be ridiculous.'

"He said, 'I don't think there's a law against it.' And I took the constitution of the New York Stock Exchange home and studied it and there was no law against women members; It had just been policy. And I met the requirements and that was it."

It sounded easy but hadn't been. In 1967, she applied for membership in the exchange. By that time, she'd become a partner in a leading New York brokerage firm and made a lot of money. Membership required a sponsor. Nine of the first ten men she asked to handle her application turned her down. "So," she said, "I couldn't be sponsored from the floor and had to take a partner, two upstairs partners, as sponsors. But it didn't change anything. It just meant maybe I was reaching too high."

Before Stock Exchange chiefs would consider her for membership, a new condition was imposed: A bank must give her a letter agreeing to loan her $300,000 of the near record price, $445,000, of her membership.

But the banks told her they wouldn't lend her the money unless the Stock Exchange agreed to admit her. After overcoming that double bind as well as additional roadblocks thrown up to stop her, Siebert was elected to membership on December 28, 1967.

"Once I got there," Siebert said, "there were a lot of things that weren't nice and a lot of things that were great. I had to deal with some people who were hostile and others who were very nice and you never knew which one was going to be which."

Muriel Siebert—friends call her Mickie—also is remembered as the first discount broker. A framed copy of a page one article in the Wall Street Journal, May 2, 1975, told that story. The day before—now remembered in financial circles as Mickie's May Day— a new federal law had abolished fixed commissions for brokers. A full-page ad by Muriel Siebert and Co. Inc., which ran later, announced as of that date, it was a discount commission house. The ad pictured Siebert cutting a hundred dollar bill in half with scissors.

Wall Street didn't approve. Her long-time clearinghouse dropped her instantly. The Securities and Exchange Commission said that unless another house could be found to clear her transactions within 60 days, her firm would lose its accreditation. Siebert asked for and received a 30-day extension and found another clearinghouse before that deadline expired. In spite of the fall-out, from the very beginning she'd been extraordinarily successful in the new world of discount brokering.

"In those days," recalled Siebert, "I could pick up the phone and if it was busy in the order room—and I used to have a glass wall where I could see the order room—I'd go in and give quotes and write orders.

"People would say, 'Isn't that Miss Siebert? Aren't you the owner?'

"I would say yes—they could tell my voice. 'And you're taking my order?'

"And I'd say, 'Yes I am sir.'

"But I don't do that anymore either. Nowadays, the machines have gotten so complicated, I'd have to study how to use the entry because each of our brokers has a machine that's hot—goes right to the floor of the exchange."

Siebert jumped up and dove for the dog running past—"Monster Girl!" She grabbed at a white packet in the dog's mouth. "You've got pepper. That will hurt your stomach, you damned dog."

The dog, a fluffy, tiny, and animated Yorkshire terrier, was followed by Eleanor. She and Siebert cornered Monster Girl and Eleanor carried the dog out.

Siebert's career seemed always to have been colorful. In 1987, she'd lobbied for installation of a women's restroom on the seventh floor of the New York Stock Exchange, site of the luncheon club where she was a regular. When nothing changed, she warned the exchange chairman if she didn't see a ladies' room on the floor by December, her 20th anniversary as an exchange member, she'd arrange for a Port-O-San to be delivered. A telephone booth went and a ladies room duly arrived.

Siebert obviously hadn't mellowed nor lost her flair for the big gesture. "Muriel Siebert's Declaration of War" read the top-of-the-page headline in The New York Times [1] a few weeks before the interview. That time, Siebert railed against aggressive competitors in the discount brokerage business. She'd described them as "used car salesmen" in the story and went after them, in greater detail, in ads beginning that week.

So where had all of this begun?

"Oh my. Childhood." Siebert rolled her eyes. "I grew up in Cleveland, Ohio. I have a sister who's older. My father was a dentist. I liked to play tennis, do those things. I was not a reader. If I have a talent, and it's always been there, it's that I can look at a page of numbers and they light up and tell me a story. I came to New York December 1954. I had dropped out of college (Case Western Reserve University 1949-1952). My father was dying of cancer and it was a long, hard death. Three years with nurses around the clock and he died broke.

"I'd say both my father and my mother had big influences on me. They were totally different kinds of people. My mother was hoping I'd get married and stay in Cleveland and have some children."

Siebert came to New York because nothing interested her in Cleveland and in those days, there were no challenging jobs open to women.

"You were either a teacher or a nurse," she said. "So I came to New York first. A lot of young people in Cleveland came to New York then. They still do. I thought I'd stay three months and then go home, but I got active and, maybe, as Thomas Wolfe said, 'You can't go home again.'

"I applied at the United Nations for a job first. I wasn't accepted because I didn't have two languages. I applied to Merrill Lynch and the interviewer said, 'College degree?' I said, 'No.'

"I applied the next day to Bache and Company. They asked, 'College degree?' I said, 'Yes.'

"They offered me a job at $65 a week as a trainee in research or $75 a week in the bookkeeping department and I took the job in research.

"I started to progress so fast that it was fun. I also made some friends in New York pretty fast. I volunteered at the Henry Street Settlement House and was active. And there were bright, young people on Wall Street. New York is a wonderful city when you come here. At that time, there was a lot to do for nothing or very little money and I really enjoyed myself."

Siebert looked at some point in the distance and shook her head: "It's incredible when I think about it. On summer weekends, we'd jump in my used Studebaker and drive to the Hamptons and you could rent a room in a house for $4 a night each if two shared the room, or $5 if you wanted a single. And that included breakfast. We went to the public beach and it was terrific. There was theater too. Tickets were reasonable if you sat upstairs and that didn't matter. Free concerts. A lot of free everything. One weekend you could drive up to Connecticut; another weekend, we'd drive someplace else. New York is just a terrific place."

She believed she'd achieved success rapidly in New York because of what she accomplished.

"I think people saw someone who was pretty good. And," she said, "I was lucky. Each of the half dozen senior analysts, industry specialists, at Bache and Company was allowed to dump one industry on a new trainee.

"So the man who had railroads and shipping—everything that moved, airlines, boats, buses—dropped the airlines on me because he didn't think they could pay for the planes they were going to have to order.

"The man who had chemicals and drugs kept these and gave me radio and motion pictures and television because to him that was a small industry compared to what he had. I wrote the first study on the value of films for television. When you write that, with your initials on it..." Siebert's eyes rolled.

"And I wrote some of the first studies on the airlines because here again was a case of numbers—the depreciation on the planes and the ability to pay off the debt and the cash flow and everything. So I was lucky in getting those industries. I've often wondered—if I'd gotten the food industry, or the utility industry, what would have happened? And you're a trainee. You don't ask for anything. They give it to you and you say, 'Yes sir.' I also had closed end investment trusts. They didn't do me any good. So I was lucky.

Muriel Siebert (Provided by M. Siebert)

"I regarded it as a serious game. I'd see a challenge and I'd say, 'I can do that.' And I'd reach and I did it. I stumbled a couple of times, but you reach and you do it and you're not allowed to make the same mistake twice.

"I changed jobs three times because they were paying men 50 percent more than they were paying me. When you're making $12,000 and they're making $19,000, that's a quality of life. That's the ability to buy a new car, to take a vacation, do what you want. When I found another job, I'd pick up my pencils and leave.

"I got my first order by accident. An institution called and said, 'We made money on a report you wrote. We owe you an order.'

"I went to the partner in charge of research and I said, 'Madison Fund called and they said they owe me an order. Should I wait until I get registered? Because I do not have a license to sell stock.' He practically shoved me out the door, 'We'll make it up to you at Christmas,' he said.

"And I started to bring in institutions because I was very active in the New York Society of Security Analysts. They were not paying me what they were paying the men, and we were doing the same business. How did I find out? Things get out in companies. And so I started to look for another job. One of the men—he'd been teaching at Harvard and fell in love with the market—came to work as an analyst and he went to one of the partners and said, 'It's not fair and she's looking for another job.'

"So they called me in. They said something like, 'We think you should get a raise,' and I said, 'You know, I feel like I'm working in a fish market and have to bargain.' The senior partner got up and looked at me. He said, 'Pay her what we owe her,' and walked out.

"Those were not nice days. But they probably gave me the strength to do in life what I wanted to do. I had that confidence of being able to move on. If you're at the same company for 10 years, you may not get that confidence.

"I don't know that I had any career goals. I was doing well and making progress and when you do well and make some progress you can buy yourself a new car—not another used Studebaker—and you can go to Europe. It opens up a life."

Siebert's next major career move was into government. In 1977, Governor Hugh Carey appointed Siebert Superintendent of New York State's Banking Department.

"I happened to be a moderate Republican and Carey called me and he's a Democrat," she said. "He told me, 'I made a commitment to hire women, and I'd like a woman to be superintendent of banks and yours is the only name that keeps coming back.'

"When you're spoken to that way, what do you say? 'When do I start?' It was work, but it was an honor." Employees of her firm took over its management.

Those were bad years for banks. Interest rates kept rising and bank failures became common across the country. To prevent bankruptcies in New York State, Siebert forced banks to merge, persuaded stronger institutions to help weaker ones, reorganized troubled banks and demanded drastic measures to keep them afloat. One bank president had his salary cut by half—by $100,000.

She persuaded the federal government to advance millions of dollars to make new mergers viable and extracted special rulings quickly from regulatory agencies not usually known for speed.

Her official resume noted that she often reminded those she dealt with that her title, Superintendent of Banking, came with appropriate initials—S.O.B. But the bottom line was, not one bank in the state failed.

On the first day of the Iran hostage crisis, Siebert phoned the state's banking examiner and told him to immediately start monitoring Iranian bank assets. She then set up a complex system of controls to protect banks from possible Iranian default.

She resigned from her government post in 1982 to run for the Republican nomination for the U.S. Senate.

"I came in second in a three-way primary," Siebert said. "I was beaten by the right-to-life candidate. They sent out a mailing and called me a baby killer because I was pro-choice.

"Any mistakes? Everyone makes mistakes. You can't NOT make mistakes. I should have run for office again. I believe in public service, and I just think this country is getting screwed. We're sending the wrong people to Washington."

Siebert's day usually begins with an automatic wake-up at 5 a.m. She works until the newspaper arrives at 6. Her apartment is a few blocks from her office and she owns a condominium in the Hamptons.

"I don't have a typical day," she said. "I do spend time in the office, but I'm more productive out of it. This morning was the television screening. I'm on the business council of the Metropolitan Museum and I'll be there at 4. We have a Women's Forum from about 5:30 to 6:30 and then I have a dinner appointment, a dinner party."

Many other groups claim her time as well. She's vice president of the New York Council of Boy Scouts. Board memberships include the New York State Business Council; National Council of World Affairs; Women in the Senate and House, a political action group; the Tokyo Advisory Committee of New York's sister city program; Alliance of American and Russian Women; and Minority and Women-Owned Business Enterprise.

An awards list is even longer. NOW, the Anti-Defamation League, Los Angeles County—even the Veuve Clicquot vineyards in Paris—were among those who saw her as the best of whatever the criteria.

When not working, Siebert enjoyed tennis, concerts and time with friends. Earlier, she'd learned to fly and thought someday she'd go back to that. She had no retirement plans. "I'll keep going until I get bored," she said. "I had an uncle who worked until he was 95. Remarkable. I take pride in what I do and as long as I'm enjoying myself, I'll work."

Another reason to stay is because she believes what she does wouldn't be done by someone else.

"We're the only woman-owned firm that can do certain kinds of business in the country," Siebert said, "that's some of the corporate underwritings we get into, and we get into that because we're a woman-owned firm.

"And I have this program where I donate 50 percent of the commissions. I find that a challenge. These ran, to date, close to $4 million. I want to get that up to $5-to $10-million a year. That's my goal. To do that means moving five times as much as we do—building a distribution."

Donations are through the Siebert Entrepreneurial Philanthropic Plan, established in 1990: That gives charities half her firm's net profits from new securities underwriting. The plan allows issuers of securities, or institutional buyers of new issues, to name any charities they wish as recipients of the SEPP donation.

Siebert personally started another fund in Los Angeles. "Our donations there have been about $350,000," she said. "I gave a hundred percent of our earnings on Chrysler and also on General Motors because I decided I didn't have to make money on every trade that went through the firm. And the California Community Foundation administers this fund pro bono.

"We make no-interest or low-interest loans to women- owned firms that were impacted in the riots and more recently the earthquakes. PBS did a half-hour program on three, four, of the beneficiaries."

One of these, a black-owned bakery making sweet potato pies, paid off its first loan and has been given a second. The current loan will pay for the larger oven necessary after the bakery won a contract to supply a Southern California supermarket chain.

"What had happened," Siebert said, "was California has a 5 percent setaside for women, and I had benefitted because we execute common stock orders for them. I wasn't just going to take the money and put it in my pocket and say, 'Thank you, Lord, I'm entitled.' I was going to share it. And because I'm doing it not to make money, but to prove a woman-owned firm can compete, can perform professionally,

"If I don't do it, there's no one downtown to do it. There are no black-owned firms doing it, but some of them..." Monster Girl streaked past, yipping. "...are doing things in other ways. I decided when I get into a deal like PacTel, our commissions were 450,000 bucks..."

Monster Girl circled the room, barking all the way.

"...we donate half after paying clearing costs," Siebert continued. "I still make a hundred thousand on the deal. So did I have to make three hundred thousand? I don't think that's the purpose of the affirmative action.

"Sure not everybody sees it that way. As one flea said to the other flea, 'To itch his own.'"

Eleanor retrieved Monster Girl. Siebert said, "We have to take her in for her nails, Eleanor. She's catching them in the rug. I hear it."

Eleanor picked up a white packet from the rug near the door. "Who's dropping the pepper all over?" Siebert asked her.

To us, Siebert said, "My vet told me when he dies, he wants to come back as my dog."

No, Siebert said, she'd never married. "I've been close a couple of times. I guess when you've been as active as I am, it would be very hard to be married. Maybe some of the younger people can do it now, but you couldn't do it then. I think I moved ahead in so many different directions that unless someone is moving ahead equally with you, it's tough."

Had she been involved with the women's movement during the 1960s and 1970s? "When it started," she said, "I was not active per se. But I became a role model and I have been very active—not in the women's movement as such, but when it really came about in 1970, I'd already become a member of the Stock Exchange.

"I think the movement was a little radical at first, but I don't think it could have started or would have had the clout if it hadn't been. These things have to start in a radical way.

"I think (the women's movement) has given women a choice: 'What do you want to do with your life?'

"I think it's created some confusion, too, since people want to do everything and they can't. And at first, there was the picketing and the whole thing, but I believe it did what it had to do—it sensitized people. But I think corporations in America still need more sensitizing.

"I happen to think women are our country's secret weapon. If we did not have the educated women in the work force, we all would be second class citizens. And without them, we could not compete on a global basis."

How would a young woman today get started in finance? "There are a lot of avenues," Siebert said. "Depends on where your talents are. Women are starting money-management firms. That's wonderful. If somebody gives you a million dollars and at the end of the year, it's a million-two, you've beaten the S and P (Standard and Poor index) by 50 percent and they don't care if you are black or white or Chinese or a woman or if you have two heads.

This is something to define your performance. And it's not a capital-intensive business to start.

"Women are also beginning to own some decent size firms where they're making good money and that's a field that's beautiful for women.

"We don't have them in the executive suites of Wall Street firms yet. Eventually, sure. But it's long overdue. We don't have blacks and other minorities in executive suites yet either. It's not happening. I don't see them on the trading desks. I don't see them in mergers and acquisitions where the big dollars are made.

"They're being treated equally as security analysts. When you look at the institutional investors, the team of 100—the hundred best at whatever they do in the industries—women are probably half of them. We're starting to see women as portfolio managers and earning money for institutions. Then they leave to start their own firm and they've got a chance to develop a very good business."

Through her various skirmishes with the power structure, Siebert learned attitudes simply don't change easily nor often. In the months and years after she'd broken the men-only barrier on the Stock Exchange, she'd found it wasn't that members didn't like her, personally, they liked the status quo.

"Things are still status quo," she said. "They just haven't changed to the right degree. I've got a lot of good friends, and I'm highly respected. I stand up and I'm counted, but when you look at it, after 27 years, it really hasn't changed all that much.

"When I got my seat, one of the governors asked me how many more women were behind me. For 10 years I could say, '1365 men and me.'"

1 The New York Times, Sunday, November 6, 1994.

16

Palma Formica, born 1928; physician; professor Robert Wood Johnson Medical School;
department head St. Peter's Medical Center,
New Brunswick, N.J.; member Board of Trustees, American Medical Association.

In the hospitals, some doctors said, 'Why isn't that woman at home, taking care of her kids?' That hurt," recalled Dr. Palma Formica during the morning interview. "But growing up poor, going to school—if every hurt knocked you down, you'd never get up. I knew who I was and what I had to do. And I got to be president of the staff. They didn't. I sit in this chair. They don't."

Formica's chair in St. Peter's Medical Center in New Brunswick, New Jersey, was behind a door labeled, "Chairman, Department of Family Practice."

Formica's resume had been an intriguing mix of the exotic and prosaic. She'd worked her way through the male strongholds of professional associations to win election to the 12-member Board of Trustees of the American Medical Association in 1990 and was reelected in 1993. Besides being a professor at the nearby Robert Wood Johnson Medical Center, she sat on many committees there.

She still practiced family medicine in her home town of Old Bridge, New Jersey, though her office was no longer a solo opera-tion. Six other doctors, all women, practiced there as well. She continued to make school calls as the physician for the town's school system. That was bare bones. The activities connected with all of that filled nine pages in her resume.

St. Peter's, a complex of parking lots and modern, multi-floored, many-windowed buildings separated by landscaped strips, sprawled across a hill above the commercial center of New Brunswick.

One room off a heavily traveled, third-floor hospital corridor was Formica's; another adjoining, her secretary's. Furniture and humming electronics crowded both offices. Papers and folders covered Formica's desk. A videocassette, "The Battered Woman," anchored a corner collection. Awards, honors, thanks and appreciation certificates filled the wall above shelves with more books and papers and family photographs.

Formica wore a dark suit, a round-necked, butter-colored silk blouse, and a string of pearls. Thick, dark hair, lightly streaked with gray, framed a large face with strong features and unlined, golden skin. When she talked, she leaned forward on her forearms, hands clasped on the desk in front of her. Her voice, deep and unfaltering, reinforced an impression of substance and sureness.

Formica grew up in Johnstown, Pennsylvania. "My father came over when he was 20 and he had a fantastically thick Italian accent," she said. "When he met my mother, he'd been on his way home to find a wife but was told he didn't have to go to Italy to find a nice Italian girl—my grandfather had 10 daughters.

"We grew up in an Anglo neighborhood. Mom and Dad never spoke Italian to us because it was wartime and they didn't want the neighbors to think they were anti-American.

"We weren't poor, we'd lived through the Depression, but we weren't rich either. My father was a part-time stone mason and a union organizer back in the days when organizers didn't get paid but could get their heads bashed in for being a part of a labor movement. I used to go to meetings of the steelworkers union with him. Johnstown was near the mines so the United Mine Workers were around there, too.

"My father was extraordinary. I think he was an American before he ever got here. He believed in democracy and his work with the union was to have a say in what working conditions were going to be.

"He believed being male or female didn't make any difference. This was America. We could do anything we wanted to do and he would assist us in doing it if we just worked hard enough. He was a hard taskmaster though. I'd bring home all A's and he'd want to know, 'Aren't they giving out A-pluses?'"

Involvement in community, school, and church was something he promoted with his four children—Palma was the oldest—and his wife.

"My mother only went to the eighth grade because she'd had to take care of the other children in her family," Formica said, "but he encouraged her to become secretary-treasurer of the community's Italian-American organization—it wasn't even in their by-laws that women could be members."

For as long as she could remember, Formica knew one day she'd be a doctor. Her inspiration may have been the physician who saw her through scarlet fever. "I'd been quite ill," she said. "We had no money, but he would come every night, teaching my mother what to do to get me through it. And at the time I was going through the crisis, he slept in our house.

"I had an aunt who was only three years older than I. Mom and Dad were better off than her parents and they would buy us dolls at Christmas time. My aunt still has those dolls. Mine didn't make three months because I cut them apart to see what was inside. I never played house unless I could be the doctor and someone always had to be sick—very sick. I only wanted to be the doctor. Not a nurse, though people tried to talk me into that because that is what women do. I said no.

"In junior high school, our homeroom teacher said what did I want to do?

"I said, 'I'm going to be a doctor.'

"She pooh-poohed me in front of the class. 'How can you, whose father is only a laborer, be a doctor?'

"I said, 'I didn't say I want to be a doctor. I said I will be a doctor.' My mother's brother also tried to convince me not to go on with this, that Mom and Dad couldn't afford it. When I got out of high school, he said, I should just get a job at the local five and dime."

Scholarships helped out. She entered the local branch of the University of Pittsburgh and lived at home for all but her senior year. When she moved to the main campus at Pittsburgh, she earned room and board as a live-in baby-sitter.

"I graduated in two and a half years and was 20 when I finished," she said. "The (World War II) veterans were coming back and in those days there was no hesitation in telling women that medical schools weren't for them, but at the same time, the Italian schools had begun accepting students from the U.S."

Post-graduate study in a foreign language sounded formidable, but Formica said it hadn't been too difficult. She'd had a good background in Latin and Italian wasn't all that different. She also knew German and French.

"It was," she recalled, "a good experience in that I was the same age as my father when he came to America, and I'd suddenly become the foreigner."

She graduated from the University of Rome in 1953 and came back to intern at Queens Medical Center in New York City.

In Italy, the concentration had been more on books and study than on hands-on practice. "So," Formica said, "I opted for a city hospital where you got lots of experience." Queens Medical Center, a 1,200-bed hospital, had been set up for 34 residents. With only 16 that year, the job came with built-in experience.

"I started the first of January," she said. "I remember my first day as an intern. I walked down the ward to surgery. The chief resident in surgery saw me coming. He said, 'Oh my God. Formica is a woman.' So that's how we started.

"And it was a day when there'd been a lot of accidents, a lot of dying people. Every place I went in the hospital, someone was either dying or in the process. I felt like the grim reaper. I thought, 'Here I am, New York, strange hospital, don't know anyone; Formica's a woman;' There would be that battle to fight, and I'd just come from Italy where half the class were women.

"Later, in my room, I asked myself, 'What did I get into? What do we do? Just sign death certificates?' And that was in the mid-1950s when we didn't have all that many wonderful things to do for people."

Residents at Queens received board and room—as the only woman Formica was assigned to nurses' rather than residents' quarters—earned $20 a month and were delighted because most hospitals didn't pay residents.

"My father would ask me, when am I coming home? I'd say, 'I can't afford it.' He would say, 'But you're a doctor.'

"I worked very hard. I tried not to have any of them have anything to say about Formica being a woman. In fact, when someone was sick and we'd have to fill in the surgical residency, the one who said, 'Formica's a woman,' always asked I be assigned. He knew I'd be there and when I was there, I'd do all the work.

"The residents had come from all over the world. We just had a great comradeship. Because there was so much to do, and everyone was so over-burdened, we simply helped each other. If I was on call, or had a lot of patients I'd admitted during the day and a great deal of work, one of the residents would say, 'Let me give you a hand.' No one left the hospital without knowing that the person left behind, doing the work, was not overwhelmed."

Formica met her husband—John Rihacek—at Queens. "He worked parttime in the X-ray department," she said. "He was the one you had to go to get the X-rays out. None of the guys could get them, but I could go down with a list this long and say, 'Gee, I need these right away.'

"We got married. I had my first son who came with a certificate for nine months of residency training en utero—I think he became a lawyer just to get even. In those days a regulation said you had to leave your job if you were six months pregnant. So I just stayed six months pregnant for the last three months and carried scissors and cord ties.

"They knew I was more than six months, but they needed me and I needed them. In those days, you didn't get credit unless you put in a whole year and if I left, I would have lost that entire year."

When it came time to set up a medical office, she had no money and a husband still in college. She took a year and a half off, gave birth to their second son, and researched where and how to begin her practice of medicine. She knew she didn't want to work in New York and she discussed other possibilities with a priest friend.

"He asked if there were any general areas that sounded good and I said New Jersey might be a nice place since that seemed to be where the growth and development was. He wrote to 88 pastors in New Jersey asking if they needed a physician in their area. Sixty wrote back and said, 'Please come.'

"We went to one of the towns and couldn't afford it and then to Old Bridge where a priest had handwritten 12 pages of demographics for us. He took us all over the area, found a house and introduced us to the bank and I became part of this new, developing community.

"When I came to town in 1959," she continued, "I had been trained in internal medicine. I called the nun who was here at St. Peter's and she told me, 'We don't need any more hotshots. What we need are doctors who can take care of families in their own localities.' At that time, I was on my way to being a hotshot specialist and instead, I went back to pediatrics and got some more training."

Old Bridge grew as she watched. World War II veterans, eager to resume their lives, wanted families and homes of their own. When Formica visited Old Bridge that first time, she saw one established development and another being built nearby. In between the two she bought her house and opened her office. She estimated the new section wouldn't be completed for five years, but a year later, all the houses had been built, sold, and occupied.

"It was an area of many young people and young families," she said. "Homes were modestly priced. The original buyers of our house, I believe, paid $10,000 for it. We paid $15,000."

She grinned. "I'm still in the same place and it's falling down around me. Workers are there right now—repairing and fixing. My sons—I've got two, one a doctor, one a lawyer, my daughter is an artist—say, 'What do you need this house for?'

"I tell them, 'See that yard out there? I may never get there, but it's my yard and where you grew up.' It's also adjacent to my office property so when they were growing up, we were just across the yard from each other."

When Formica opened her office, her shingle was intentionally genderless—P.E. Formica, M.D. That was by way of a hedge because she believed that once a patient, male or female, came into her office they'd be back. In a short time, her practice included as many men as women patients.

"There were seven other doctors in the larger area and what we soon did, which pleased me, was take turns working weekends so we weren't working seven days since all of us were young and we all had children. They'd asked me to join them. For me, that was acceptance by my peers."

Formica laughed. "My father came to visit. I was busy, so I'd say, 'Daddy, I have to make house calls. Get in the car and we'll talk on the way.'

"One night he said, 'I thought I do a good thing. I work-like-a-hell to make you a doctor and now you work-a-like hell.'"

No, she said, it hadn't been all roses those early years. Though patients fully accepted her, others in the community had reservations.

"I'd applied for a car loan," she said, "and was told I needed my husband's signature because New Jersey was a community property state. That was a month after my husband bought a truck I did not sign for, did not want him to buy. I went back to the bank with all my papers—my ledgers with liabilities and assets. And the bank officer said, 'Well, no. It's a policy.' At that point it became the principle of the thing.

"Earlier, when I'd gone to them to buy my property, they wouldn't give me the loan so, when I got to the car, it was the second slap. I'd wanted that property, but my husband said he didn't think it was a good idea. I said I want it and I'm going to have it. So I incorporated. "The realty company had said as a corporation I could buy the property on my signature: as an individual I couldn't. I went back to the bank with all those statement things. They said, 'No. It's company policy.'

"'Look,' I said, 'I've paid off three cars with your company and it's obvious my salary can carry a business car. Plus I have this other property.' No.

"'You'll hear from me,' I said, 'and you'll hear from my lawyer.' But I didn't call the lawyer. Instead I called the president of the bank. I said, 'I'm a productive member of the professional community and none of my physician friends had to have their wives sign for their business cars and I don't think I have to either.'

"The next thing was this telephone call asking me to come in and sign the loan papers. Then a letter arrived saying they'd transferred the manager, though mine was not a bad case (of discrimination) because I was a young woman."

What being a young woman actually meant, was "What if you get pregnant? You'd have to stop work." That had been a common question—and the answer—in many women's professional dealings. She learned later that a judge had asked for a $5,000 loan to make up the difference between what she had and the price of a new Mercedes. The only way she got the loan was with a cosigner, her 86-year-old father.

From the beginning, Formica said, "I had a very, very active family practice and I always believed we needed more family physicians, even way back then. When the medical school (then Rutgers, now Robert Wood Johnson) decided to start a residency program, they came to me and asked me to bring my practice there as the base for their program."

The Catholic sister who was then the administrator of St. Peter's promoted the plan and since the university hospital had no room and little real interest in a family residency, this began at St. Peter's. Formica is associate director of the university's program which began in 1980 with one resident. The department now has 70 family physicians with 24 residents, and remains based at the hospital.

Oh yes, she said, she continues to see many, many patients at her Old Bridge offices. "I'm still in private practice. Absolutely.

"When we started our residency program, one of the things we incorporated was, you can't teach how to be a family doctor unless you are still a family doctor. It's fine to know all of the theories, but unless you are in that one-to-one relationship—and now with the health system changing as it is, unless I know what my fellow physicians are going through, then I am just another hireling who is trying to be in the system without being part of it."

When Formica began directing the residency program at St. Peter's, less than 10 percent of the full professors in the 126 U.S. medical schools were women. According to a federal survey, that percentage remained the same in 1995, though the number of women med students grew to 42 percent. In 1995, only four medical schools had female deans and less than five percent of their department heads were women.

Formica believed that women didn't move into administrative positions at the same rate as male colleagues because the biological urge to have children peaked during the years of medical school.

"They then get put on a clinical track which means they don't have the research opportunities," she said. "There's not enough mentoring. Women aren't aggressive enough. I started out as an assistant professor of clinical family medicine (University of Medicine and Dentistry of New Jersey) which is the teaching track, not the tenure track. At the time I was delighted to be asked."

Palma Formica

At the end of 10 years, she'd become a full professor, but not effortlessly. She learned at some point a colleague with the same credentials came in higher, at an associate level. Formica took classes in negotiating before confronting administrators with her new knowledge. "When it became time for promotion, they remembered me," she said.

Her residency program also stresses patient responsibility.

"In our daily interaction, we are continually feeding them how we think things ought to be done," she said. "For instance, a resident was supposed to meet me at school yesterday to do school physicals and she forgot. I said to her, 'I'm old enough to be your grandmother and I don't forget my appointments. It's your responsibility to be where you are supposed to be. If someone says we're meeting at 8 o'clock, we meet at 8, not 8:10 or 8:15. Just because we're physicians doesn't mean we have the right to keep someone waiting. If I'm running late, I don't take lunch.'"

Formica encourages leadership, too.

"I find that women haven't been socialized to take that step," she said. "Despite our having been through the women's movement, most of the women I run into have been hesitant. When they say, 'There are no role models in leadership positions,' I say, 'When there aren't, you have to be. You use that to create initiative to take that step.' Through all the organizational things I've been involved with, a leadership role didn't come because I sat there and looked pretty. It was having the initiative to do things because I thought they were right.

"My job here—chair of the department—was going to be given to someone else. Given. But it's an election process and I said, 'We have to have an election. The rules state that and I put my hat in the ring.' That was in 1972.

"And I became the director of a nursing home because there, too, it was supposed to go out for bids since it was a county facility. They were simply going to pass the director's post on to someone else. I said the job must go out for bids. So they then had two applicants and I got the job. I believe things have to be done a certain way, within the system."

Assuming leadership, she continued, simply means being aware and looking around—what needs doing? When Formica came to Old Bridge, the town had no well-baby clinic for those families who couldn't afford routine check-ups and shots for their children plus basic information. The clinic she started, she explained with a wry grin, was by then so well established, family practitioners were no longer employed, only pediatricians.

"You have eyes," she said, "you can see, and you have a responsibility to that greater community to respond to where the needs are. Many of the things I did, I did because I believed someone had to present the other side—what the people needed—not the politician's side."

Formica became involved with the American Medical Association for that reason.

"Now I can bring my experiences and what my patients need to a level where policies are made and where you can influence policies," she said. "Being a physician is a great honor, but it comes with a lot of responsibilities and accountabilities.

"I believe that physicians are the servants of the people, and in leadership I subscribe to the idea that leaders are servants. We are not there for power or to shake hands with Hilary."

That was not a figure of speech. In a photo on the wall, a couple of feet from where she sat, Formica, in an official-type setting, shook hands with First Lady Hillary Rodham Clinton.

In 1979, the AMA membership agreed there would be no discrimination against women physicians in any professional activities. "We were trying to get the Equal Rights Amendment through," Formica recalled, "but the guys were not buying it. So what we did was submit the words of the Equal Rights Amendment as a resolution, but didn't call it that.

"In hearings on this, doctors would stand up and say, 'I don't know of anyone being discriminated against.'

"I would stand up and say, 'Here I am. Let me tell you what happened to me at the bank.' They passed it. It took two years, but they passed it."

As a result, Formica became a member of the AMA's ad hoc committee on women and medicine.

Her professional affiliation had begun at a local level with the county medical society.

"I'd been very involved with the community and with my church," she said, "and in 1960, I'd worked with a group on sex education for the public and parochial schools.

"That had involved a lot of talks before different civic groups. I was in the hospital lunchroom one day and one of the guys said, 'I see your name in the paper all the time—giving a talk here and there. How come you're not involved with the medical society?' I said, 'Who would want to be a part of that male chauvinist organization. Ha Ha.' That evening I got a telephone call from the nominating committee. Would I please be the reporter—that's like a secretary—for the county medical society? I said, 'No. I'm too busy.' He said, 'Pam, put up or shut up.' Since nobody is going to shut me up, I took the job."

As a member of the local medical association, she saw where she could influence policy and move things ahead for patients and also for women physicians.

No woman had ever been president of the county's medical society. Not until Formica worked her way there—through the system. She volunteered for jobs rather than waiting to be asked. When she was appointed alternate delegate to the state convention in Atlantic City she accepted, thinking that would be a vacation spot her children would enjoy. The following year she attended as a delegate. Next step was the state society's board of trustees; after that, president of the oldest state medical association in the country.

"When the guys said, 'How wonderful it is to have a woman as president'—once they take that major step, everyone is terribly happy about it—I'd remind them it took 222 years before they got it right."

Formica's second term as trustee on the American Medical Association board would end in 1996. Trustees are limited to three, three-year terms. Formica planned to stand for a third term and would again be in contention with ten others for four vacancies. She'd been through that before. The first time she ran was in 1984, at a time when women's participation at top levels was being encouraged.

"There was another woman running that year," Formica recalled. "I was dumb. I was honored to be asked. When you're running against two or three men and another woman, they're not going to take both women, but I wasn't smart enough to figure that out. I didn't get enough votes to elect half a dog."

Losers traditionally and publicly congratulate winners. Formica did that and announced, "I'll be back."

The predominantly male house, she'd learned, respected those who lose and come back. Prior to the 1990 race, she'd made personal calls to many delegates, asking for their support. One said to her, "We've already elected a woman to the board (the first was Dr. Nancy Dickey the previous year). How many do we have to have?" "How many seats are there on the board?" Formica asked.

After a solid win, she wrote personal cards of thanks to everyone. "I paid my dues. They appreciated the fact. I don't think you can come on like gangbusters. You have to make them laugh, not take yourself too seriously.

"I grew up in a generation of women that got what we wanted by making other people think it was their idea. As long as the outcome is what you're looking for, it doesn't matter who gets the credit. I sometimes wish that some of my young sisters would know that you can still get more with honey than with vinegar."

Formica's memories of the women's movement of the 1960s and 1970s was of a radical group, detrimental to the quiet revolution that she saw working very well.

"If we had gone to the good old boys medical societies and tried to push our way in," she said, "we'd probably still be sitting outside. But we worked with them, let them know our goals were the same as theirs. The women's movement did raise awareness, but it also turned people off.

"Many of us in many different fields worked our way up, dedicated to the fact that it's not important to be the only woman who gets there. We can't have the Queen Bee syndrome. Unless others follow in the pipeline, it's just a shot in the dark. We have to facilitate and share what we've learned with those following us. I had mentors in the professional societies, so I must mentor other people. I believe I've done that with men and with women, but I find the need greater among women. They are not as aggressive nor as assertive and I can relate to that. I remember walking into a room and being the only woman and afraid to open my mouth because the others would look down their noses at me.

"But I decided when I had something important enough to say, it was important people heard it. In spite of a ball in my stomach, I learned to walk in like I owned the world. That's what the guys do."

Other events in her life had been more difficult than that. At 50, after a long illness, her husband died.

"He was not a man you could tell what to do," Formica said. "I would make appointments for him and he would break them. Though he'd been a medic in the service, culturally he believed if you went to a doctor, they would tell you something bad. If you went to a hospital, you would die there. He was admitted to the hospital with a perforated intestine. So the guilt—what should I have done? Should I have seen that?"

For the last half year of his life, her husband was paralyzed from the waist down. His final three months he was hospitalized. Not until a week before his death did he admit he had cancer.

"I learned to appreciate a patient's values," she said. "You say you have empathy, but until you've been through it, you don't really know."

Though Formica disliked the odd aches that accompanied aging, getting older really didn't disturb her. "I've earned it," she said. "I'll practice until someone tells me I shouldn't and I have friends who have promised they would tell me. Sometimes we don't realize. But my father was 96 when he died; my mother is 85 and her mind is in good order."

Formica's days are long, the nights short. "At a time when I could be slowing down," she said ruefully, "I no longer have my major place of operation in my backyard. It's 10 miles from there to the hospital and I'm in my car, commuting, every morning."

She travels frequently for AMA purposes and mostly likes it, particularly when she's on stage because, she said, "I like to talk."

She called the AMA the most democratic organization she'd been involved with. Being one of 21 trustees had given her a look at the other side, she said. It is the board that implements policies determined by the 400- to 500-member house of delegates. A current focus was educating physicians to recognize domestic violence. A 1995 study reported 35 percent of women admitted to emergency rooms were victims.

If she lost the 1996 election, what then? She grinned. "There is life after the AMA." She had a list ready: a visit to relatives in Italy; back to oil painting; reading "light stuff;" classical music; opera.

"I said to my kids, when they talked about what they wanted to do, 'Find what you like doing and they will pay you for it.'

"I've liked my life. Sometimes I get a bit tired of traveling, hotels, hotel food, but it's all been fun. And for some of this, the enjoyment and personal satisfaction, I've been paid and much better than my father ever achieved in his lifetime."

17

AFTERWORDS

A majority of the women in this book earned college degrees. During the years when they were students, women routinely prepared themselves to work in traditional fields. Obviously, this has changed. To learn how counselors guide women today, I wrote to career offices in universities and colleges attended by the women interviewed.

The following provided information: Dr. Barbara Reinhold, Smith College, Northampton, Massachusetts; Jack Tinker, Connecticut College in New London; Marilyn Bowles, Mills College, Oakland, California; a spokesperson from Vassar College, Poughkeepsie, New York; Dr. Jaems E. Scales, Southern Illinois University at Carbondale; Jean Hernandez, University of Washington, Seattle.

All agreed they no longer channeled women into studies for role-traditional careers such as nursing and teaching. Some, however, believed women continued to make different career choices than men based on what they perceived to be female aptitudes and futures.

Scales said females tended to doubt they would be able to compete successfully in male-oriented areas such as engineering, sciences, and math. Bowles mentioned women's expectations of family responsibilities. Tinker believed family and relationship issues complicated career plans for some women. He wrote of one who planned to pursue a 9 to 5 medical practice in pediatrics, rather than an unpredictable specialty such as obstetrics, so she could better organize a family life.

Hernandez said as long as women continued to be the primary caregivers, their ability to stay focused on work issues would be affected.

So some of the old conflicts remain. How do women balance personal ambitions and personal relationships? No good answers exist to that. Every women finds her own way. Just as we read in these pages.

Up until the 1960s, the study of men was thought to be totally appropriate for the study of mankind. No one ever thought that strange at all. But, thank goodness, that's changed. The University of California at San Diego introduced the first full Women's Studies program in its 1970 fall catalogue. By 1974, colleges offered 2,000 women's studies courses; by 1982, that had jumped to 30,000. *Peterson's Guide to Four-Year Colleges* (1996) lists 220 colleges and universities in the U.S. and Canada with majors in Women's Studies. Mills College was among the first, according to Bowles.

The University of British Columbia's Centre for Research in Women's Studies and Gender Relations is chaired by Gillian Creese. She wrote that 1996 was the fifth year that UBC, in Vancouver, had offered a degree program in Women's Studies and the 25th year of related courses.

A sampling of the latter is representative: Introduction to Gender Relations; Women's Studies in the Social Sciences; and Women in Comparative Perspective.

Of particular interest to women of my generation was Reinhold's note that in 1995, her office worked with 9,000 alumna.

I Can't Do What?

"We see women returning to Smith for encouragement to go back and pick up dropped threads from their past," she wrote. "Just last month I helped a 53-year-old woman with applications to a physician's assistant program. Where they start out has very little relevance to what they'll be doing at the ends of their lives."

* * *

I would hope that this book will inspire and motivate the women who read it, no matter their ages or the circumstances of their lives.

The 16 women who told their stories came from as wide a range of backgrounds as it is possible to imagine. Some were born into wealth, others raised in poverty. Many of their families were supportive, a few grew up in families with serious problems.

These women lost individuals important to them. They survived life-threatening illness.

Some women had long and satisfactory marriages; others were widowed, divorced, or remained single.

A few knew at a young age what work they would do; more found encouragement and guidance from their teachers. Still others didn't launch their careers until late in their lives.

Faith Hubley had something to say to all of us. She grew up in New York City's Hell's Kitchen, with family problems that led her as a teenager to consider suicide. Her husband died, she fought cancer for many years. Money remains a problem despite her successful career making films. She pretends there's funding and begins. Catalogues of her work and Oscars in her living room prove that's good enough.

Iona Campagnolo grew up in the farthest remote reaches of British Columbia, worked in a salmon cannery and married a fisherman. She was 33 and the mother of two when she realized she was "capable of doing many other things than society in the 1950s accorded women." Jean Payne began a successful career at approximately the same time in her life.

In 1970 Anne Wexler was a housewife running a political campaign. Eight years later she worked in the White House.

Vi Hilbert began teaching at the University of Washington when she was 54. Until then she'd owned and operated a beauty shop. In 1994, the National Endowment for the Arts recognized her as a Master Artist.

Daughter of a banker, Katherine Fanning married wealth and left it in Chicago to begin again in Alaska.

Florence Robinson faced death. Part of her recovery was deciding to be true to herself, to become the individual she'd discovered she was.

Newly arrived in the United States and a student, Denise Scott Brown survived a car crash which killed her young husband.

Patricia Wald's family was poor. Scholarships took her through college and law school. After marriage she took 10 years off to raise five children.

June Biedler flunked out of Vassar: Caroline Herzenberg flunked kindergarten.

Evelyn Foote and AhQuon McElrath worked their way through college. Both found their way into uniquely male fields. Neither are, or ever were, at all reluctant to speak out on controversial issues.

These women came out of the lottery of birth and circumstance with the same mixture of positives and negatives issued to all of us. They worked from the same listings of available options.

Many of us wonder at various watershed moments of our life if we can take a path that both lures and awes. Some of us will turn away and for the rest of our lives regret our decision. The women in this book chose the difficult way.

Their voices speak to those of us who still dream of taking a path less traveled.

INDEX

A

Aaron, Hank, 179
Academy Awards, 30
A Century of Women in America, 186
Aero Insurance Underwriters, 156
affirmative action, 109, 209
African Women's Studies, 81
age range, of interviewees, 7, 10
aging, 31, 58, 60, 78, 95, 127, 149, 161, 177, 226
AIDS, 82, 137
Aid to the Aged and Blind, 185
Aid to the Disabled, 185
Air Force, 49, 83, 155, 174
Alaska pipeline, 68, 77
Albert, Eddie, 22, 23
Allen, Clinton, 129
Alliance of American and Russian Women, 208
Alumay, 47
Alzheimer's, 83
Amazonia, 32
ambition, in women, 12, 143, 167, 166
American Acad. of Arts and Sciences, 125
American Airlines, 54
American Association for Cancer Research, 139
American Association of University Professors, 51
American Bar Association, 10, 125
American Bar Assoc. Foundation, 125
American Battle Monuments Com., 174
American Law Institute, 125
American Medical Association, 10, 54, 212, 222-224, 226, 227
American Society of Newspaper Editors, 66, 76
American University, 52
Anchorage Daily News, 66, 68-70
Anchorage Times, 68, 69
*Animated Women,*15, 20
Annecy Film Festival, 28
Antheil, George, 26
Appollo explorations, 140, 144
Architectural Assoc., London, 97-99
Argonne National Laboratory, 140, 141, 143, 146, 149
Army, 10, 11, 77
Army Command and General Staff College, 166
Army War College, 165-167
Arnold, Thurman, 117
assasinations, 13
Atlanta University, 79, 80,
Atwood family, 68, 74-76

B

Bache and Company,203, 204
Bail in the United States, 119, 126
Baldwin, James, 91
Barbour award, 161
Barry, Marion, 115
Bazelon Center, 121
Bazelon, David, 121
Bell, Griffin, 122
Bernstein, Leonard, 88
Biedler, June, 128-139, 233
Big Bang and Other Creation Myths, 30
birth control, 10
Bishop College, 90
blacklist, 24
Blue Cross, Blue Shield, 164
Bonnard, Pierre, 26
Bork, Robert, 115
Boston University, 76
Bowles, Marilyn, 228, 229
Brico, Antonio, 87
Bridges, Harry, 182
Brown, Denise Scott, 96-110, 233
Brown, Robert Scott,98, 99
Brown vs. Board of Education,126
Bryant College, 47
Bush, George, 54, 199
Butkus, Dick, 179

C

cabinet, Canada, 35
California Community Foundation, 209
California State Univer. at Fresno, 145
Callaway family, 79, 81-83
Camera on Science TV series, 147
Campagnolo, Iona, 11, 33-46, 232
Camus, Albert, 57
Canadian Native Arts Foundation, 42
Canadian politics, 36

cancer, 27, 68, 131, 133, 134, 137, 196
Cannes Film Festival, 28, 30
careers—changes, 7, 8, 228, choice of, 7, 8, 10, 11, 14, 36, 203, 210, 211, 228
Carey, Hugh, 206
Carter, Jimmy, 47, 50, 51, 53, 54, 57, 116, 122, 199
Case Western Reserve University, 203
CBC-TV,40
Center for Foreign Journalists, 77
Center for Law and Social Policy, 120
Center for Sustainable Regional Development, 45
Chaplin, Charlie, 24
Charles Stewart Mott Foundation, 77
Chicago Daily News, 67, 68
Chicago Herald-American, 86
Chicago Sun-Times, 67, 68
childhood, 25, 26, 31, 33, 34, 48, 61-64, 67, 83-86, 107, 112, 113, 129, 142, 153, 154, 171,172, 180, 188, 203, 213, 214, 215
Christian Science Church, 67, 69, 71, 77
Christian Science Monitor, 66, 69-72, 76, 77,
Cine Golden Eagle, 28, 30
Cinematique, 23
civil liberties, 184
Civil Liberties Union, 144
Civil Rights Act, 114
civil rights movement, 13, 91, 168
civil service, 11, 189
Civil War, 8, 80
Clark-Atlanta University, 79, 81
Clark College, 80, 91
Clarke, Mary E., 168
class distinctions, 33, 38, 42
Clinton, Bill, 48, 49, 52, 54
Clinton, Hillary Rodham, 223
CNN, 186
Cochran, Jacqueline, 155, 160
Columbia College, 25
Columbia Studios, 22, 23, 25, 26
Columbia University, 128, 132
Comcast Corporation, 47
Commission on Status of Women, 9
Congo, 92

Connecticut College, 116, 228
Conservative party, Canada, 42
Cornell University, 128, 132
correctional facilities
see Payne, 187-197
Cosby, Bill, 80
Cosmic Eye, 30, 31
Curie, Marie, 143, 144
D
Dartmouth College, 103, 198
Day, Doris, 9
death, 29, 64, 69, 84, 99, 158, 196, 226
Defense, Department of, 168
Democratic, 1968 convention,119
Democratic National Committee, 50
Denver, cultural complex, 103
Denver Public Schools, 88, 89, 92
depression, 20, 67, 144
Depression, the, 7,9, 11, 112, 171, 180
Dickey, Nancy, 225
Dinkins, David, 198
Disney, 17, 24
divorce,36, 39, 49, 67, 90, 120
DNA, 129, 130, 132
dogs, 57, 199, 202, 209, 210
Dole, Robert, 54
domestic violence, 226
Doonesbury, 29, 30
Dos Passos, John, 48
Douglas, Helen Gahagan, 8
Dreiser, Theodore, 48
Dreyfus, 47
Dubois, Rene, 132
DuBois, W.E.B., 80
Duffey, Joe, 49-52, 56, 57
Duwamish, the, 59
Dvorak, Antonin, 20
E
Education for All Children Act, 121
education, higher, 12, 36, 42, 47, 48, 65, 67, 87, 88, 91, 92, 97, 116, 129, 130, 132, 133,141, 154, 164, 181, 188, 191, 203, 215
Eiffel Tower, 106
Emory University, 82
employment, 15
Enter Life, 30

Environmental Protection Agency, 114
Equal Pay Act, 8
Equal Rights Amendment, 91, 122, 223
ethics, business/professional, 55, 78,
124, 125
Etude, 88
F
Family Crisis Intervention Unit, 191
Fanning, Katherine Woodruff, 66-78,233
Fanning, Larry, 68, 69, 73, 76
FBI, 164
federal courts, 176, 178
Feminine Mystique, 9
feminism, 28, 39, 100
Ferraro, Geraldine, 52
Field, Marshall, Jr.67, 68, 73, 76
Fifth Amendment, 185
Finian's Rainbow, 24, 27
First Nation people, 34, 35, 38
Flight Safety Foundation, 156, 157, 160
flying clubs, 152
Foote, Evelyn, 11, 163-178, 233
Fordham University, 137
Formica, Palma, 212-227
Fortas, Abe, 117
Fort Belvoir, 163
Fort McClellan, 165
Frank, Jerome, 117, 122, 123
Freed, Dan, 118
Freedom Forum Media Study Center, 77
Freedom of Information, 114
Friedan, Betty, 9
G
garden clubs, 11, 37
GATT, 55
General Motors, 54, 77,
Georgetown University, 125
George Washington University, 172
Gershwin brothers, 95
Geyer, Georgie Anne, 73
GI Bill, 188
Ginsberg, Ruth Bader, 115
Go Man Go, 24, 27
Goodwin, Richard, 50
Grayline, 164
Great Books, 67
Gulf War, 169

H
Haight Ashbury, 191
Hall, Jack, 181
Hankinson, Will, 35
Harlem Globetrotters, 23
Harvard, 50, 66, 96, 198, 206
Hawaiian mythology, 19
Hawaiian Pineapple Company, 182
Hawaiian Tuna Packers, 182
Health and Human Services, department
of, 51, 114
Health, Education and Welfare, depart-
ment of, 51, 182
Heath, Gloria, 151-162
Hecht, Ben, 26
Hello, 30
Hell's Kitchen, 25
Henderson, Fletcher, 80
Henry Street Settlement House, 203
Hernandez, Jean, 228, 229
Herzenberg, Caroline, 140-150, 233
Herzenberg, Leonard, 143
Hess, Thom, 61, 65
Hidden Cities, 48
Hilbert, Don, 58
Hilbert, Violet Anderson, 58-65, 232
homosexuality, 176-178
House Appropriations Committee, 54
House Un-American Activities Commis-
sion, 24, 185
Houston Film Festival, 31
Houston Museum of Fine Arts, 103
Howe, James Wong, 24
Hubley, Faith, 17-32, 232
Hubley, John, 18, 20, 23, 24, 27-32
Human Reproduction, 22
human rights, 42
I
Illinois Institute of Technology, 143, 148
illness, 27, 28, 60, 65, 89, 90
Industrial Revolution, 8
In Quest of Cookaboody, 28
Institute for Global Ethics, 77
Institute Gustave-Roussy, 133
International Academy of Astronautics,
141, 158-161
International Civil Aviation Organiza-

tion, 156
interviewees, 230, 231—expectations of, 11, 22, 36, 49, 62, 67, 87, 98, 113, 130, 134, 143, 154, 165, 166, 188, 203, 214, 215, 231—selection, 10, 11
Iran-Contra, 115
Italian-American Organization, 214
J
Japanese-Canadians, 33-35
Jim Thorpe, 103
Johnson and Johnson, 54
Johnson, James Weldon, 80
Johnson, Lyndon, 9, 49
Jordan, Hamilton, 50
journalism, 10, 13, 15, 164
K
Kahn, Louis, 89
Kaiser Foundation, 213
KCTS, 15
Kennedy, John, 9
Kennedy, Roger, 48
Kennedy, Robert, 116, 118
Kennedy School of Government, 50
Kettering, Charles, 131
Kettering Foundation, 77
Korean War, 117
Korn, Arthur, 98
L
labor market, 8-9
lacrosse, 138
Landers, Ann, 73
Law and Poverty, 119
law, importance of, 126, 177
leadership, 41, 44, 53-55, 70, 71, 82, 136, 170, 175, 195, 222, 224, 225
Learning from Las Vegas, 101, 102
Legal Aid, 120
Legal Services, 119, 120
Lewis, Sinclair, 48
Liberal Party, 35, 37, 38, 40-43
libraries, 25, 112
library science, 81
life changes, 12, 13, 36, 60, 67, 89, 90, 132, 188
Lipstick Building, 199
Los Angeles Times, 71
Lowry, Mike, 64

lunar samples, 138, 144, 148
Lushootseed, 59, 61, 64
M
Madeira School, 129, 130, 138
management skills, 55, 70, 71, 82, 170, 184, 193, 221
Mandela, Nelson, 82
Manhattan Project, 146
Maraniss, David, 49
Margo, 22
Marquis Who's Who, 10
marriage, 11, 12
Massachusetts Institute of Technology, 141
Mathews, Mo, 66, 67
Maynard Institute for Journalism Education, 77
McCarthy, Eugene, 49
McCarthy, Joseph, 24
McClatchy Newspapers, 69, 70
McElrath, AhQuon, 179-186, 230
McElrath, Robert, 181, 182
medals, military, 163
Memorial Sloan Kettering Cancer Center, 128, 130, 131, 133, 135, 136, 138
Memphis, downtown plan, 103
Mental Health Law Project, 121, 122
Metropolitan Museum, 207
Mickie's May Day, 201
military, 9-11,
Military Leadership, 167
Mills case, 121
Mills College 187, 189, 194, 228
Minority and Women-owned Business Enterprise, 208
models, women as, 10-12, 15, 175, 176, 208, 222
Morehouse College, 80
Morehouse School of Medicine, 80
Morris Brown College, 80
Mossbauer, 143, 144, 148, 149
mythology, 20
N
National Aeronautics and Space Administration, 144, 159
National Assoc. of Women Judges, 125

National Council of World Affairs, 208
National Endowment for Arts, 58, 60
National Endowment for Humanities, 51
National Gallery, London, 102, 104
National Heritage Fellowship, 58
National Institutes of Health, 137
National Labor Relations Board, 114
National Maritime Union, 184
National Museum of American Indian, 102
National Org. for Women, 9, 208
National Park Foundation, 47
Native American Languages Act, 59
Native Americans, 19
Navy, 168
NBC, 29, 30
New Brutalism, 98
New Deal, 117
New Guardians of the Press 68
New Masses, 181
New York Council of Boy Scouts, 207
New York Society of Security Analysts, 206
New York State Banking Department, 206, 207
New York Stock Exchange, 153, 198, 200-202
New York Times, 18, 71, 116, 198, 202, 211
New York University, 198
Nickerson, Eugene, 178
Nixon, Richard, 93, 119, 199
Norman, Jimmy, 142
North, Alex, 23
North, Oliver, 115, 126
Northwestern University, 88
Notre Dame University, 125
nuclear power, 141
O
Oahu Sugar Company, 183
Oakland Raiders, 192
O'Keefe, Georgia, 23
Oliphant, Patrick, 56
Oscars, 17, 32
Osteoporosis Society, 45
P
Parliament, 35, 37

Payne, Jean, 11, 187-197, 232
PBS, 17, 45, 82, 88, 89, 92, 93, 140, 147, 209
Pease, David, 25
Pentagon, 168, 175, 176
personal philosophies, 31, 45, 56, 64, 79, 106, 107, 127, 139, 150, 162, 184, 186, 190, 173,05, 221, 222
Peterson's Guide to Four-Year Colleges, 229
Phi Beta Kappa, 116
pilot's license, 145, 151, 142, 160, 208
political defeats, 40, 207
Porter, Paul, 117
President's Commission on Crime, 119
President's Commission on Law Enforcement, 119
Price, Florence, 95
PTA, 185, 196
Pulitzer Prize, 69, 76
Putney School, 153, 154
Q
Queens Medical Center, 215, 216
R
racism, 24, 38, 42, 83, 85, 92
Rainbows of Hawaii, 18
raising a family, 39, 40, 76, 89, 108, 118, 119, 146, 185, 189, 218
Reagan, Ronald, 51, 54, 199
recreation/hobbies, 31, 45, 56, 107, 126, 145, 146, 161, 174, 177, 208, 227
Reinhold, Barbara, 228, 230
religions, 32, 62, 63, 67, 71, 77
Republic Studios, 26
retirement, 15, 56, 61, 77, 78, 94, 127, 139, 149, 175, 177, 227
Reynolds, Bertha, 184
Rhodes University, 36
Rice University, 96
Robert Wood Johnson Medical Center, 212
Robert Wood Johnson Medical School, 212
Robinson, Florence Crim, 79-95, 233
Robinson-Pattman Act, 118
Rockefeller, Lawrance, 156
Rockefeller University, 132

Roe vs Wade, 10
Rolling Stone, 47, 50
Roosevelt, Franklin, 117
Ross, Bob, 137
Royko, Mike, 73
Rubenstein, Anton, 26
Rutgers University, 219
Rye Country Day School, 129
S
St. Peter's Medical Center, 212, 213, 217, 220
San Francisco Chronicle, 68
Scales, Jaems, 228, 229
Schlafley, Phyllis, 174
Schmoe, Floyd, 15
scholarship, 36, 86, 113, 142
scholarships, 113, 117, 215
Scouts, 11
Scripps-Howard newspapers, 164
Scuria, Antonin, 115
Seattle Art Museum, 102
Seattle University, 58
Second Chance: Sea, 28
Securities and Exchange Commission, 114, 117, 201
Seeger, Charles, 98
Seers and Clowns, 30
sex discrimination, 9, 34, 38, 46, 75, 101, 109, 143, 166, 167, 170, 176, 190, 200, 200, 201,205, 206, 211, 215, 216, 218, 219, 223
Shaker Church, 62
Shippensburg State University, 163
Shriver, Sargent, 119
Siebert Capital Markets, 199
Siebert Entrepreneurial Philanthropic Plan, 208
Siebert, Muriel, 198-211
Simon Fraser University, 46
Skagit culture, 58, 61, 64
Skidmore College, 47, 49
Sky Dance, 30
Sloan, Alfred, 131
Smith College, 66, 67, 73, 151-154, 184, 228
Social Security Act, 181
Society of American Physical Society, 146
Southern Illinois University, Carbondale, 79, 83, 85, 88, 90, 228
South Street Project, 103
Spanish-American War, 142
Spanish Civil War, 181
Spectre of the Rose, 26
Spelman College, 80
Standard and Poor, 210
Starlore, 30
Starr, Ken, 115
State University of New York, 140
Statistical Abstract, U.S., 15
status crimes, 191
Step by Step, 30
Stevenson, Adlai, 49, 95
Stokowski, Leopold, 26
Strategic Defense Initiative, 147, 148
Strauss, Robert, 50
strikes, 24, 182
suicide, 26
Supplemental Security Income Act, 185
Supreme Court, 10, 89, 124, 125
T
Tall Time Tales, 17
teachers, as mentors, 11, 25,48, 85, 86, 87, 98, 116, 129, 142, 172, 180
teamwork, 54, 70, 71
Thatcher, Denis, 39
Thatcher, Margaret, 39
Thomas, Clarence, 115
Three Mile Island, 141, 146
Time of the Angels, 30
Tinker, Jack, 228, 229
Tokyo Adv. Committee, Sister City, 208
Trudeau, Gary, 30
Trudeau, Pierre, 39-41
Turner, John, 42, 43
Twain, Mark, 92
U
United Mine Workers, 213
United Nations, 203
United Productions of America, 23, 24
United States Courts of Appeals, 111, 114, 115
United States Information Agency, 52, 164

University of British Columbia, 230
University of California, Berkeley, 99, 187, 188, 191
University of California, San Diego, 196, 229
University of Chicago, 140, 141, 143
University of Colorado, 88, 89
University of Denver, 88
University of Georgia, 82
University of Hawaii, 181
University of Illinois Medical Center, 45
University of Massachusetts, 51
University of Medicine and Dentistry, New Jersey, 220
University of Northern British Columbia, 38, 44, 45
University of Pennsylvania,96, 97, 99, 100, 103
University of Pittsburgh, 215
University of Rome, 215
University of Virginia, 65
University of Washington, 58, 61, 228
Upside Down, 30
USA Film Festival, 31
Utah State University, 146
V
Vassar, 25, 128-130, 133, 138, 228
Venturi and Rauch, 100, 101, 103
Venturi, Robert, 97, 100, 101, 108, 109
Veuve Clicquot, 208
Vietnam, 91
Vietnam War, 49, 172
anti-war movement, 49
Villanova University, 125
Villiers Foundation, 185
Voice of Labor, 181
volunteerism, 11, 36, 48, 67, 182, 188, 196, 207
W
WACS,163, 165, 166, 168, 176
wages earned by women, 15, 24, 124, 205, 216
Wagner Act, 180
Wake Forest University, 163, 165, 166, 168, 176
Wald, Patricia McGowan, 111-127, 233
Wald, Robert, 112, 117

Wall Street Journal, 71, 201
Ward, Margaret, 25
War on Poverty, 119
Washington Avenue development, 102
Washington Daily News, 164
Washington Economic Club, 47
WASPS, 151, 155, 160
Watership Down, 29
Way, Mary, 35, 36
Weaver, Howard, 28
welfare, 186
Westover School, 67
West Point, 165
Wexler, Anne, 47-57, 232
Wexler Group, 47, 54, 55, 57
Whither Weather, 30
White House staff, 53, 54, 57
Whitewater, 115
Who Am I?, 35, 36
Wings Club, 160
Women's Forum, 207
Women's Hall of Fame, 201
Women of the World, 28
women's history, 8, 9
women's movement, 75, 91, 137, 138, 168, 210, 225
Women's Studies, 229, 230
Wolfe, Thomas, 203
World Council of Churches, 93
World War I, 8, 142
World War II, 9, 22, 24, 34, 48, 59, 98, 116, 129, 131, 141, 151, 153, 155, 157, 158, 164,169, 174, 175, 188
Writings About Vi Hilbert, 60
Y
Yale, 96, 100, 111, 117, 118, 125, 129
Yale School of Art, 17, 25, 28
Yes We Can, 30
Yoder, Janet, 60
Z
Zagreb World Festival, 31

ORDER FORM

Pathfinder Publishing of California
458 Dorothy Ave.
Ventura, CA 93003-1723
Telephone (805) 642-9278   FAX (805) 650-3656

Please send me the following books from Pathfinder Publishing:

_____Copies of **Beyond Sympathy** @ $11.95 $_____
_____Copies of **I Can't Do What?** @ $14.95 $_____
_____Copies of **Injury** @ $9.95 $_____
_____Copies of **Living Creatively**
              With Chronic Illness @ $11.95 $_____
_____Copies of **Losers, Users & Parasites** @ $9.95 $_____
_____Copies of **Managing Your Health Care** @ $9.95 $_____
_____Copies of **No Time For Goodbyes** @ $11.95 $_____
_____Copies of **Quest For Respect** @ $9.95 $_____
_____Copies of **Sexual Challenges** @ $11.95 $_____
_____Copies of **Surviving an Auto Accident** @ $9.95 $_____
_____Copies of **Violence in our Schools, Hospitals and**
              Public Places   @ $22.95 Hard Cover $_____
_____   @ $14.95 Soft Cover $_____
_____Copies of **Violence in the Workplace** @ $22.95 Hard $_____
              Violence in the Workplace @ $14.95 Soft $_____
_____Copies of **When There Are No Words** @ $9.95 $_____
                                   Sub-Total $_____
              Californians: Please add 7.25% tax. $_____
              Shipping* $_____
                                   Grand Total $_____

I understand that I may return the book for a full refund if not satisfied.
Name:_____

Address:_____
_____ZIP:_____
Credit Card_____Card No._____
*SHIPPING CHARGES U.S.
Books: Enclose $3.25 for the first book and .50c for each additional
book. UPS: Truck; $4.50 for first item, .50c for each additional. UPS
2nd Day Air: $10.75 for first item, $1.00 for each additional item.
Master and Visa Credit Cards orders are acceptable.